Nation and Peace Without Unity
The Problem of State-building in the Context of the Ethnopolitical Fragmentation of Modern Afghanistan

Akramjon Fozilov
University of Vienna

This page is intentionally left blank.

Nation and Peace Without Unity: The Problem of State-building in the Context of the Ethnopolitical Fragmentation of Modern Afghanistan

© 2020 IndraStra Papers
IndraStra Global
162 W 72nd Street,
New York – 10023, U.S.A.
Tel: +1-516-926-0755, Email: *info@indrastra.com*
URL: *www.indrastra.com*

Some rights reserved. Published in 2020
Printed in the United States of America

Imprint: IndraStra Papers | Publisher: IndraStra Global

Commissioning Editor: Tanushri Indoria

Illustrator: Rose McReid

Cover Image: Amber Clay

ISBN: 9798666958599

The views expressed in this e-book publication are those of the authors and do not necessarily reflect the views and policies of the *IndraStra Global* or its team members or the organizations they represent.

IndraStra Global does not guarantee the accuracy of the data included in this publication and accepts no responsibility for any consequence of its use. The mention of specific companies or products of manufacturers does not imply that they are endorsed or recommended by *IndraStra Global* in preference to others of a similar nature that are not mentioned.

By making any designation of or reference to a particular territory or geographic area, or by using the term *"country"* in this document, *IndraStra Global* does not intend to make any judgments as to the legal or another status of any territory or area.

This work is available under the Gratis Open Access through Creative CommonsAttribution-NonCommercial-NoDerivatives 4.0-International-License. By using the content of this publication, you agree to be bound by the terms of this license.

This CC license does not apply to non-IndraStra Global copyright materials in this publication. If the material is attributed to another source, please contact the copyright owner or publisher of that source for permission to reproduce it. *IndraStra Global* cannot be held liable for any claims that arise as a result of your use of the material.

Attribution: In acknowledging *IndraStra Papers [Imprint]/ IndraStra Global [Publisher]* as the source, please be sure to include all of the following information:

Author. Year of publication. Title of the material. © IndraStra Papers, URL. Available under a CC BY NC ND 4.0 license.

Translations: Any translations you create should carry the following disclaimer: Originally published by the IndraStra Global in English under the title [title, author name(s)] © [Year of publication] IndraStra Papers. The quality of this translation and its coherence with the original text is the sole responsibility of the [translator]. The "English language" original of this work is the only official version.

Adaptations: Any adaptations you create should carry the following disclaimer: This is an adaptation of an original Work © [Year] IndraStra Papers. The views expressed here are those of the authors and do not necessarily reflect the views and policies of IndraStra Global or its team members or the organizations they represent. IndraStra Global does not endorse this work or guarantee the accuracy of the data included in this publication and accepts no responsibility for any consequence of its use.

Please contact info@indrastra.com if you have questions or comments concerning the content, or if you wish to obtain copyright permission for your intended use that do not fall within these terms.

This page is intentionally left blank.

This page is intentionally left blank.

About the Author

AKRAMJON FOZILOV is the master's student of the "Global Studies - a European Perspective" (Erasmus Mundus Master's course in Global Studies - EMGS) at the University of Vienna (Austria). He obtained a bachelor's degree in World Politics from the University of World Economy and Diplomacy (Uzbekistan). He served as Lead Researcher of the Information and Analytical Center for International Relations (Tashkent, Uzbekistan). He has published several books and articles concerning his research. His areas of interest: Public Policy, Conflict Resolution, Security, and Peace Studies.

This page is intentionally left blank.

Index

Sr. No:	Content	Page No:
1	**Abstract**	11
2	**Introduction**	12
3	**Theoretical Aspects of the State-building in Deeply Divided Societies**	20
	The Theoretical Understanding of Roots of the Ethnopolitical Fragmentation of Afghanistan and the Concept of "Failed State."	20
	The Classical Approaches in State Formation under the Ethnic Contradictions	33
4	**The Historical Roots and Basics of State-building in Afghanistan**	46
	Stages of the Multi-Ethnic Statehood Formation of Modern Afghanistan	46
	Drawbacks of Ethnopolitics of the Modern Afghan Government	63
5	**The Prospects of the Multi-Ethnic Political System in Afghanistan through Institutional Mechanisms**	85
	External Impact on Ethnic Relations in Modern Afghanistan	85
	Democratic Institutions and Prospects for Promoting the Mutual Interests of Ethnic Groups in Modern Afghanistan	92
6	**Conclusion**	109
7	**Bibliography**	113
8	**Appendices**	129

This page is intentionally left blank.

ABSTRACT

This research paper is devoted to studying the problems of state-building in Afghanistan in the context of the ethnopolitical fragmentation, as well as analyzing issues related to resolving the "Afghan problem," taking into account the interests of the mutually competing and mutually cooperating military-political forces of Afghanistan. The author also examines the shortcomings of the ethnic-policy of the Islamic Republic of Afghanistan and various possible ways of resolving the "Afghan problem" at the present stage. Also, the author investigated the theoretical aspects of state-building in post-conflict states (societies), the theoretical understanding of the roots of the ethnopolitical fragmentation of Afghanistan and the concept of a "failed state," classical approaches to the state formation under the ethnic conflict conditions, and considered the prospects of a multi-ethnic political system in Afghanistan through institutional mechanisms.

Keywords: *ethnopolitical fragmentation, state-building, "failed state," decentralization of power, ethnic identity, national identity, Afghanistan*

INTRODUCTION

As we are aware, one of the main reasons for the intensification of the "Afghan crisis" is some institutional issues in the government of the Islamic Republic of Afghanistan. Besides, the last suspended negotiations between the US government and the Taliban movement in Qatar shows the desire and readiness of the Taliban for an inter-Afghan dialogue, who were previously often, described as ardent Pashtun nationalists.

In this regard, the relevance of the research topic is studying the problem of state-building in Afghanistan through the prism of the interests of various ethnopolitical forces and groups. This will give the readers thorough information on possible ways of resolving the "Afghan problem" at the present stage.

Literature Review: The problem of ethno-confessional relations in Afghanistan has always been at the center of research. However, at the preparatory stage of research, quite a large amount of scientific literature was encountered, in which the dependent and independent variables of the research (*ethnic and religious relations in Afghanistan, decentralization of power, state-building in conflict, foreign intervention in ethnic conflict, consolidation of political forces based on an ethno-confessional trait, the concept of "failed states," etc.*) were examined.

In particular, various aspects of inter-ethnic conflict, ethnic fragmentation, and inter-ethnic competition within the country were subjected to research by *M.Yundina, V Avksentyev, S.Rubashkina, A.Zotova*[1]; *M.Brill Olcott, I.Semenova*[2]; *J.McGarry, B.O'leary*;[3] as well as *B.Shoup*[4]. In turn, *A.Guelke*[5] considered the problem of creating strong democratic institutions in societies (countries) affected by ethnic conflict. Issues of federalism and

---

[1] «Этнический конфликт: теория, экспертиза, пути решения». Сборник «Школа миротворческих инициатив» / Составители: М.А.Юндина, В.А.Авксентьев, С.А.Рубашкина, А.В.Зотова. Ставрополь: 2001.

[2] Язык и этнический конфликт / Под ред. М. Брилл Олкотт и И. Семенова; Моск. ЦентрКарнеги. — М.: Гендальф, 2001. — 150 с.

[3] McGarry, John, and Brendan O'leary, eds. *The politics of ethnic conflict regulation: Case studies of protracted ethnic conflicts*. Routledge, 2013.

[4] Shoup, Brian. *Conflict and cooperation in multi-ethnic states: institutional incentives, myths and counter-balancing*. Routledge, 2007.

[5] Guelke, Adrian, ed. *Democracy and ethnic conflict: Advancing peace in deeply divided societies*. Springer, 2004.

institutional solutions to the ethnic conflict in India and Pakistan, which have cultural, historical, and geographical proximity to Afghanistan, were studied by *K.Adeney*[6]. Also, the features of ethnic processes in the conditions of transformations analyzed in the studies of *A.Bragin* and *I.Maksimov*[7]. Possible ways of optimizing interethnic relations, criteria for the selection of national policy priorities are determined.

Classical approaches to state-building and the political system take place in the works of *M.Weber*.[8] Moreover, *C.Call*[9] and *R.Caplan*[10] also study the central importance of state institutions in post-war peace-building. In turn, the concept of "failed states" and the ways to solve it on the example of Afghanistan and other countries of the Middle East, Africa, and Europe are examined in the research

---

[6] Adeney, Katharine. *Federalism and ethnic conflict regulation in India and Pakistan*. Springer, 2016.

[7] Брагин А., Максимов И. «К вопросу о сущности понятия «Этнический конфликт» в условиях этнотрансформационных процессов». *Среднерусский вестник общественных наук* 2 (2009). стр. 53-62.

[8] Вебер, Макс. Политика как призвание и профессия. *Избранныепроизведения* (1990): 644-706.

[9] Call, Charles T. "Building states to build peace? A critical analysis." *Journal of Peacebuilding & Development* 4.2 (2008): 60-74.

[10] Caplan, Richard, ed. *Exit strategies and state building*. Oxford University Press, 2012.

by *N.Chomsky*[11]; *R.Gordon*[12]; *A.Ghani, C.Lockhart*[13]; *C.Call*[14]; *G.Helman* and *R.Ratner*[15].

The history of Afghanistan, concerning the historical stages of building a multi-ethnic nation, the role of a religious and ethnic factor in the political life of Afghanistan, as well as foreign intervention in the "Afghan conflict" is studied and analyzed in the works of *J.Lee*[16]; *F.Ahmed*[17] and *V.Korguna*[18]. Also, *D.Mukhopadhyay*[19] has considered the role of warlords (military-political leaders of various ethnic

---

[11] Chomsky, Noam. *Failed states: The abuse of power and the assault on democracy*. Metropolitan Books, 2007.

[12] Gordon, Ruth. "Saving failed states: sometimes a neocolonialist notion." *Proceedings of the ASIL Annual Meeting*. Vol. 91. Cambridge University Press, 1997.

[13] Ghani, Ashraf, and Clare Lockhart. *Fixing failed states: A framework for rebuilding a fractured world*. Oxford University Press, 2009.

[14] Call, Charles T. "Beyond the 'failed state': Toward conceptual alternatives." *European Journal of International Relations* 17.2 (2011): 303-326.

[15] Helman, Gerald B., and Steven R. Ratner. "Saving failed states." *Foreign policy* 89 (1992): 3-20.

[16] Lee, Jonathan L. *Afghanistan: A History from 1260 to the Present*. Reaktion Books, 2018.

[17] Ahmed, Faiz. *Afghanistan Rising: Islamic Law and Statecraft Between the Ottoman and British Empires*. HarvardUniversityPress, 2017.

[18] Афганистан в начале XXI века. Институт востоковедения РАН. Ответственный редактор: В.Коргун. М., 2004, стр. 191.

[19] Mukhopadhyay, Dipali. *Warlords, strongman governors, and the state in Afghanistan*. CambridgeUniversityPress, 2014.

groups in Afghanistan) in resolving the "Afghan problem."

The theoretical and practical significance of the research: The proposals and conclusions contained in this work can be used as a theoretical basis for the further systematic study of the problem of state-building, ethnic conflict, power decentralization, and consolidation of political forces based on an ethnic and religious character of Afghanistan.

The practical significance of the work is due to its focus on creating a generic objective view of the ethnopolitical fragmentation of the country and the political system of Afghanistan. Additionally, an integral part of the practical significance of this study is that of providing certain conclusions and suggestions for improving as well as strengthening the state system which is developed as a result of the study.

The research object and subject of study: The research object of this paper is the state of current political and social relations in the Islamic Republic of Afghanistan, which is developing with the context of the ethnopolitical fragmentation of the country and political consolidation based on ethno-confessional interests.

The research subject of the study is a set of socio-political and historical-cultural issues (processes) and factors related to the problem of state-building within the context of ethnopolitical fragmentation of modern Afghanistan and the prospects for resolving the "Afghan problem."

Research methodology and analysis methods: Methodology is a system of principles for scientific research, a set of research procedures for collecting, preprocessing, and analyzing information.[20] Consequently, the methods of content analysis, cognitive mapping, comparative, and historical analysis are used in this research to further explore the essence of the object and subject of study.

Goals and objectives of the study: In this research paper, I would further like to explore and analyze the problems of state-building under the context of the ethnopolitical fragmentation of modern Afghanistan. Therefore, issues related to the settlement of the

---

[20] См.: Ядов, В. А. Социологическое исследование: методология, программа, методы. Самара, 1995. с. 31.

"Afghan problem" will also be considered, taking into account the interests of mutually competing and cooperating military-political forces of Afghanistan.

The main tasks of the research paper are as follows:

- determine the dependent and independent variables of the study;
- to define the concepts of *"ethnopolitical fragmentation"* of the country and the essence of main conceptual issues of state-building in Afghanistan;
- study and analyze the influence of the current ethnic situation of Afghanistan on its political processes within the country, inclusive of the role of tribal relations within the Pashtun society,
- conduct a comprehensive analysis of positions and goals of the main ethnopolitical forces of modern Afghanistan;
- identify and study the problems of decentralization of power that exist in the modern system of government of the IRA;
- identify, through system analysis, proposals for improving and strengthening the

institutions of state and public administration of the IRA, taking into account current trends in the political life of the country;
- assess the course of events in Afghanistan through the prism of national interests and the current foreign policy of the Republic of Uzbekistan.

CHAPTER 1

Theoretical Aspects of the State-building in Deeply Divided Societies

1.1. The Theoretical Understanding of Roots of the Ethnopolitical Fragmentation of Afghanistan and the Concept of "Failed State."

Characteristic Features of the Ethnopolitical Fragmentation of Modern Afghanistan

To study the features of the ethnopolitical fragmentation of modern Afghanistan, we first need to consider the issue of ethnic interests in the process of state-building in Afghanistan. The achievement of the struggle in Afghanistan in the 1990s led to the ethnic conflict becoming a basic policy of the Afghan society. It embraced all the spheres of social activity. In particular, state construction, the formation of public authorities, and local government. It, in turn, had no way but led to processes which resulted in the weakness of the new government and the entire Afghan statehood. Therefore, the decentralization of power and fragmentation of the political system of the country got directly linked with the ethnic contradictions within Afghanistan.

The ethnonational confrontation primarily affected the process of adopting the Constitution, which determined its difficulties and drama. In particular, the proposed version of the presidential republic met with opposition from representatives of ethnic minorities who defended the *parliamentary form of government* and did not want to concentrate power in the hands of the president - Pashtun. Burhanuddin Rabbani headed the opposition. Hamid Karzai threatened that he would not run for president unless the Loya Jirga[21] approved the presidential form of government.[22] The result of the bargaining was a compromise, on which Afghanistan remained a

---

[21] A Loya Jirga, or "grand council" in Pashto, is a mass national gathering that brings together representatives from the various ethnic, religious, and tribal communities in Afghanistan. It is a centuries-old institution that has been convened at times of national crisis or to settle national issues. Historically, the Loya Jirga has been used to approve a new constitution, declare war, choose a new king, or to make sweeping social or political reforms.(*FrudBezhan. Radio Free Europe/Radio Liberty.* https://www.rferl.org/a/afghanistan-loya-jirga-explainer/25174483.html)

[22] Лалетин Ю. П. Межэтническое взаимодействие в Афганистане //Конфликты на Востоке: этнические и конфессиональные/Под ред. АДВоскресенского.–М.: Аспект Пресс. – 2008. – с. 289-314.

presidential republic, but the powers of the president were curtailed; he or she could not dissolve the parliament. The lower house must approve the proposed government. However, the parliament does not have the right to impeach the president.[23][24]

Nevertheless, the leaders of the opposition in the National Assembly were going to make changes to the Constitution, concerning the parliamentary form of government and the establishment of the post of Prime Minister primarily. Because of the settlement of the political crisis during the presidential election of 2014, a so-called unconstitutional post appeared - the Head of the Executive Branch (*Chief Executive* or *Prime Minister*). The primary opponent of Ashraf Ghani in the presidential election, Dr. Abdullah Abdullah, assumed this post.[25]

---

[23]Rubin, Barnett R. "Crafting a constitution for Afghanistan." *Journal of Democracy* 15.3 (2004): 5-19.

[24]Constitution of the Islamic Republic of Afghanistan. Ratified January 26, 2004. Chapter Three: The President (11 articles), Chapter Five: National Assembly (29 articles).

[25]Craig, Tim (21 September 2014). "Ghani named winner of Afghan election, will share power with rival in new government". *Washington Post*. Retrieved April 15, 2019. Available at: https://www.washingtonpost.com/world/ghani-abdullah-agree-to-share-power-in-afghanistan-as-election-stalemate-ends/2014/09/21/df58749a-416e-11e4-9a15-137aa0153527_story.html?noredirect=on&utm_term=.3fb6b1a935c6

At the constitutional Loya Jirga and during its preparation, there was a proposal about the *federal structure of Afghanistan*, in other words, transforming Afghanistan into the federation. The most energetic guides of this idea were the military-political leaders of two ethnic groups - Uzbeks and Hazaras. As early as 2002, a draft program of the National Islamic Movement of Afghanistan (*Junbish*, a political party headed by General Abdul Rashid Dostum) was published, which called for the separation of powers on a federal basis. Also, the delegates to the constitutional Loya Jirga divided into Pashtuns and non-Pashtuns on issues related to the use of national languages.

Even the presidential election of October 2004 turned into a form of ethnic confrontation. A year ago, leading military personnel and politicians of the Northern Alliance decided to nominate their candidacy. However, the case was not limited to one candidate. As already mentioned, representatives of all significant (not counting Pashtuns) ethnic groups participated in the presidential elections as candidates: Tajik Yunus Qanuni (ranked 2nd, got 16.3% of the vote), Hazara Muhammad Mohaqiq (3rd place,

11.6%) and Uzbek Abdul Rashid Dostum (4th place, 10%). During the election campaign of the lower house of parliament, many candidates spoke of unity, avoiding appeals to national and tribal feelings. For support, they turned primarily to religious feelings. However, ethnic minorities - Tajiks, Hazaras, and especially Uzbeks, supported their parties and their leaders. So, out of 20 Uzbek deputies, 19 are established by the National Islamic Movement of Afghanistan. The absence of the same absolute consolidation among Tajiks and Hazaras explained the split of their parties and factions. That goes along the line of relations with the government of Karzai.

Consequently, the House of the People (Wolesi Jirga) elected in September 2005 unevenly reflects the multinational composition of Afghan society. According to researched estimates, between 42-47% of the deputies were Pashtuns, 22-23% were Tajiks, 12% were Hazaras, 8% were Uzbeks.[26] However, deputies believed that the proportionality of national representation was violated

---

[26] Коргун В.Г. Состав афганского парламента. Институт Ближнего Востока. Режим обращения: https://www.iran.ru/news/analytics/36479/Sostav_afganskogo_parlamenta

in the executive branch. Thus, the House of the People's Commission on Justice made a statement on September 20, 2006, that Tajiks headed 53% of the highest posts in the government, and the share of the rest ethnic groups was insignificant. The document also stated that the proportionality of the national representation was violated in the Presidential Administration. The issue of the distribution of posts in the government and the proportionality of the representation of various nationalities in it has already been raised several times at meetings of the lower chamber. According to the deputy commission member from Bamyan Mohammed Sarvar Javari, as of 2006, out of 420 seats in the Presidential Administration, 72% belonged to Tajiks, 14% to Pashtuns, 4.6% to Hazaras and 0.4% to Uzbeks. In the government, 53% of Tajiks, 32% of Pashtuns, 4% of Hazaras, and 3% of Uzbeks and small ethnic groups were not represented at all. He recalled that according to the Bonn Agreements,[27] Pashtuns got 33% of the

---

[27] The Bonn Agreement (officially the Agreement on Provisional Arrangements in Afghanistan Pending the Re-Establishment of Permanent Government Institutions) was the first series of agreements passed on December 5, 2001, and devoted to creating an Interim Authority until the Transitional Authority, which was established by the emergency Loya Jirga.

seats, 24.5% to the Tajiks, 19% to the Hazaras, and 13% to the Uzbeks. Somehow, these proportions were not respected.[28]

All this indicates that the ethnic contradictions in Afghan society are profound and affect the very foundations of the government.

Theoretical Understanding of the Concept of "Failed States"

In general, we can distinguish the two different approaches to the phenomenon of "state failure":

Representatives of the *first approach* are American scientists William Zartman and Robert Rothberg. They consider the state primarily as a service provider. According to Zartman, the state can be considered collapsed, "when the main functions of the state are no longer fulfilled."[29] In other words, the state will collapse when it can no longer provide the services for which it exists. Rothberg defines state

---

[28]Лалетин Ю. П. Межэтническое взаимодействие в Афганистане //Конфликты на Востоке: этнические и конфессиональные/Под ред. АД Воскресенского.–М.: Аспект Пресс. – 2008. – с. 289-314.

[29]Zartman, I. William, ed. *Collapsed states: the disintegration and restoration of legitimate authority*. Lynne Rienner Publishers, 1995. p 5.

failure as the inability of states to provide positive political services (goods) to their residents.[30]

Both Zartman and Rothberg distinguish between the various services that states can provide: from security to the rule of law, protection of property, the right to political participation, the provision of infrastructure and social services such as health and education. Rothberg argues that these services constitute a hierarchy. Security is the most fundamental service provided by states, in the sense that security is a condition for the provision of all other services. Besides, the state may have some features (signs) of statehood, but not others. For example, a state may have a monopoly on legitimate violence, but cannot provide infrastructure or support the rule of law, or it may have armed forces, but an inefficient state apparatus. This concept is used as a guide against whom the state data is measured.

As a result of the definition of statehood in terms of the provision of services, Rothberg and Zartman believe that according to these criteria, most, if not all, states should be classified as "failed" (including Western states). After all, no state can

---

[30]See: Rotberg, Robert I., ed. *When states fail: causes and consequences*. Princeton University Press, 2010.

perform all the functions assigned to it. The limited statehood of weak, broken, or failed states considered a problem that needs to be solved.[31]

Nevertheless, the concept of Zartman and Rotberg "the state as the main supplier of services," and the model proposed by them can be used as a standard (model) - what the state should look like. Thus, for Rotberg and Zartman, the absence of certain features related to statehood is an argument in favor of changing the political system and institutions of governance in various countries of the world to fit the concept of statehood.

According to the *second approach*, a failed state is a state that cannot control its territory and support the rights to legal violence. This approach is presented, in particular, by theorists of International Relations Robert Jackson[32] and Stephen Krasner[33]. In this context, the term "failure" does not merely refer

---

[31] Eriksen, Stein Sundstøl. "'State failure'in theory and practice: the idea of the state and the contradictions of state formation." *Review of International Studies* 37.1 (2011): 229-247.

[32] Jackson, Robert H. *Quasi-states: sovereignty, international relations and the Third World*. Vol. 12. Cambridge University Press, 1993.

[33] Krasner, Stephen D. "Sharing sovereignty: New institutions for collapsed and failing states." *International security* 29.2 (2004): 85-120.

to the inability of a state to perform the functions assigned to it. Instead, the term applies precisely to the inability of the state to control its territory and monopolize the use of legitimate violence.

Jackson states that after the end of colonialism, all states are recognized as equal participants in international relations. Thus, all states have external (or unfavorable) sovereignty in the sense that they are recognized by other states as states, participate in international organizations, and establish diplomatic relations with other states. They are subjects of international law and have the right to conduct their internal political actions without external interference.

At the same time, in many states, there is no positive sovereignty as stated by Jackson. They do not control their territory. They may encounter armed rebels and have very few opportunities to promote economic development. Nevertheless, they persist and continue to be recognized as participants in the international system. Jackson and Rosberg[34] argued that this recognition was the only reason why weak African states continued to exist altogether: since such

---

[34] Jackson, Robert H., and Carl G. Rosberg. "Why Africa's weak states persist: The empirical and the juridical in statehood." *World politics* 35.1 (1982): 1-24.

recognition gives the state access to foreign (international) aid. In other words, international recognition allowed states to continue to exist, even if their actual control over their territory was minimal. Jackson describes such states as "quasi-states"[35]. He argues that a quasi-state is a state, which is recognized by subjects of international relations but does not possess empirical characteristics of statehood, such as a monopoly over the means of legitimate violence and control over its territory.

Like Jackson, Krasner focuses on the institution of sovereignty and international relations. According to Krasner, modern sovereignty consists of three components:

- The *first* is *legal sovereignty*. That is the recognition of the sovereignty of one state by others. The essence of legal (international legal) sovereignty lies in the fact that legal recognition represents the opportunity to be a

---

[35]See: Jackson, Robert H. *Quasi-states: sovereignty, international relations and the Third World.* Vol. 12. Cambridge University Press, 1993.

participant in international relations and enter into voluntary agreements.[36]

- *Secondly*, sovereignty can be understood as the exclusion of the right of external actors to interfere in the political decision-making process of the state. It means that a sovereign state does not depend on all external forces and that no external actors have the right to interfere in the decision-making process of a sovereign state (the principle of non-*intervention*).
- *Thirdly*, sovereignty means the position of the state as the highest political power on its territory (*internal sovereignty*). A sovereign state determines the rules that all members of society must follow. To be sovereign in this sense, states must have a monopoly on the means of legal violence and control over its territory.

---

[36]See: Krasner, Stephen D. "Sharing sovereignty: New institutions for collapsed and failing states." *International security* 29.2 (2004): 85-120.

Consequently, "state failure" is a condition of a state, which is determined by the absence of one or various other factors mentioned above. In this regard, the concept of "failed states" is much narrower than in the first approach. Additionally, in this approach, there is no definition of the state as a service provider. However, the meaning of both points of view is that any deviations from their respective definitions of statehood can be assessed as a disadvantage. That is, since most countries, even though they have total power over the entire territory of the country, they have specific deficiencies in the provision of services or have limited control over their territory. Consequently, according to this approach, many developing countries can be considered "failed."

1.2. The Classical Approaches in State Formation under the Ethnic Contradictions

Considering the classical approaches to state-building in the context of ethnic contradictions in Afghanistan, the following essential points (factors) should be taken into account:

First, the population of Afghanistan consists of several large and small ethnic (ethno-confessional) groups, none of which is dominant, given the share in the total population. Also, one of the reasons for the country's ethnopolitical fragmentation is the fact that despite the three hundred years old history of the Afghan statehood, the "Afghan nation" in the socio-political sense of this term has not been formed. That is, almost all ethnic groups of the country have ethnic identity prevailing over national identity. Consequently, this also aggravates the ethnopolitical processes inside Afghanistan. We now turn to the theoretical understanding of the issue of "ethnos-nation":

Ethnos, an ethnic group - in some theories of ethnicity, a historically established stable set of people united by common objective or subjective signs, in which various authors include origin, a single language, culture, economy, territory of residence, self-consciousness, appearance, mentality, and more.[37] In turn, a *nation* is a type of ethnos; historically emerged a socio-economic and spiritual community of people with individual psychology and self-consciousness.[38] There is no single approach to the definition of this incredibly complex phenomenon. Representatives of psychological theory see in the nation a cultural and psychological community of people united by a common destiny.

The most significant supporters of the materialistic concept emphasized the commonality of economic relations as the basis of the national community. One of the classics of modern sociology, P. Sorokin, considers the nation to be a complex and heterogeneous social body, an artificial construction without its substance.[39] Part of the researchers among the essential features of the nation called the familiar

---

[37]People, James; Bailey, Garrick (2010). *Humanity: An Introduction to Cultural Anthropology* (9th ed.). Wadsworth Cengage learning. p. 389.
[38]Anderson, Benedict. *Imagined communities: Reflections on the origin and spread of nationalism.* VersoBooks, 2006. p. 43.
[39] См. Сорокин П. А., Согомонов А. Ю. Человек, цивилизация, общество. – Изд-во полит. лит-ры, 1992. – с. 272.

territory, economic relations, language, history, culture, and identity.

The formation of a nation is objectively related to the formation of states. Therefore, K. Kautsky considered the national state of being the classical form of the state. However, the fate of every nation does not connect with statehood; instead, it is a perfect coincidence. According to the concept of K. Kautsky, commodity production and trade were the most critical factors for consolidating people into a nation.[40] Most modern nations were born in the process of folding bourgeois relations (from the 9th – 15th centuries), but they were formed and developed before capitalism.

In countries where development has been stalled for centuries by colonialism, this process continues to the present. The last three decades of the 20th century marked by the emergence of national statehood on the wreckage of pseudo-federal and allied states.

The second factor is that the Afghan state has always been associated with Pashtuns, as the "titular ethnicity of Afghanistan". Of course, this was because

---

[40] Каутский К. О материалистическом понимании истории. – Основа, 1923. с. 89.

when Ahmad Shah Durrani created the first Afghan state (Durrani Empire) in 1747, the population of this state consisted mainly of Pashtun tribes. However, when in the second half of the 19th century, the Pashtun rulers finally captured Afghan Turkestan and Hazarajat (Hazarestan), the Pashtuns were no longer the dominant ethnic group in Afghanistan. To preserve their power over the northern regions of Afghanistan, the rulers of Afghanistan carried out the ethnic expansion of Pashtuns into Afghan Turkestan and Hazarajat, creating "Pashtun enclaves" in these territories. At the same time, Tajiks, Uzbeks, and Hazaras became outsiders in the political system of Afghanistan before the Saur revolution (1978). All of this hurt inter-ethnic relations in Afghanistan.

If we proceed to this question from a theoretical point of view, it should be noted that ethnic groups are subject to changes in the course of ethnic processes - consolidation, assimilation, expansion, etc. For a more sustainable existence, an ethnic group seeks to create its own social and territorial organization (state).

Ignoring the Multinational Character of Afghan Society

Besides, it should be noted that the inter-ethnic confrontation in Afghanistan has found its reflection even in the academic circles of Afghan society. Today there are several historical works whose authors deny the ethnic diversity of the population of Afghanistan. In their works, they focus on the outstanding features of the Pashtuns and the exceptional role they played in the development of Afghan statehood.

For example, in the late 1930s, Professor of the Kabul University Najibullah in his work called "Ariana or Afghanistan" stated that all the people (considering all ethnic groups) of Afghanistan are "Afghans" and constitute a "United Afghan Nation". The author called all the states that existed in antiquity and the Middle Ages (before the formation of the Afghan state in 1747) "Afghan" and also stated that the Afghans (meaning Pashtuns) should assume the historical duty for the material and spiritual culture created by the joint efforts of all the people living in Afghanistan.[41]

---

[41] See: T. Najibullah, *Ariana yo Afgonistan. Ta'rihi muhtasare Afgoniston* (Ariana or Afghanistan. A Short History of Afghanistan), Al-Azhar, Peshawar, 1379, pp. 12-20.

Other Afghan scholars believe that only Pashtuns are the indigenous people of Afghanistan, and all the rest (non-Pashtun communities) are "newcomers". Some scholars are trying to distort history and claim that "a few Pashtun tribes" are Tajiks. Others claim that Tajiks, Uzbeks, Turkmen, and other ethnic groups inhabiting northern Afghanistan appeared after the conquest of Central Asia by the Russian Empire, the establishment of Soviet power, and the civil war (at the end of the 19th century in the first quarter of the 20th century).[42]

An attempt to distort historical reality is still ongoing even today by the representatives of the Pashtun diaspora abroad. For instance, the Pashtun scholar S.Afgan, in his work *"The Second Sakao"* (published in Pashto by the Center for Afghan Culture in Germany) considers the entire history of Afghanistan of the 20th century from the position of the great Pashtun chauvinism and ignores the existence of non-Afghan people. S.Afgan also defines the tasks of preserving the national unity and territorial integrity of Afghanistan. He also supports

---

[42]Abdulloev, Rakhmatullo. "Influence of the ethnic factor on the formation of Afghan statehood." *Central Asia & the Caucasus (14046091)* 15.1 (2014).

the traditional demands of the Pashtun nationalists to recognize all citizens of the country as "Afghans" and to make Pashtu the only official language.

To ensure the security of the northern regions, he proposes to create a "security belt" from the Pashtun tribes of the southern, southeastern, and eastern provinces along the border regions with Tajikistan, Uzbekistan, and Turkmenistan, as well as around the most important cities and means of communication.[43] The author also claims that the Panjshir Valley in the last century has become a stronghold of resistance against the rest of the population of Afghanistan. In this regard, he proposes to withdraw the Tajik population of the valley and resettle the place for Pashtun tribes.

It should be noted that attempts at direct falsification of historical reality aimed at enhancing the role of the Pashtun tribes in the socio-political and cultural-civilizational history of Afghanistan. However, not only in modern studies but even in the historiographic works of the 19th century, we can face the historical reality. For example, the famous German geographer Karl Ritter (1779-1859) in his

---

[43] S. Afgan, *Sakavii duvvum* (The Second Sakao), Dorulnashr, Kabul, s.a., p. 156.

research, divided the population of Afghanistan into three categories:

1) Afghans (Pashtuns), who are the majority of the population of Afghanistan. Nevertheless, Ritter asserts that they are not the indigenous (autochthonous[44]) population of the entire territory of the country;

2) The people who inhabited the territory of Afghanistan before the conquest of Pashtuns: Tajiks, Swati, Gindki, and Siahpushi.

3) People who came to Afghanistan with different conquerors in different historical times: Arabs, Kyzylbashi, Indians, Armenians, Jews, Hazaras, and Chagatai Turks (Uzbeks).[45]

In his work "The Development of Feudalism and State Education among Afghans", the well-known orientalist Igor Reisner (1898-1958) proved the illegitimacy of the assertion of several Afghan historians about the exclusive role of the Pashtuns. He stated that in the 11th century (and later), the Tajiks

---

[44]Inhabiting a place or region from earliest known times; aboriginal (*Collins English Dictionary*).
[45]РиттерК. ЗемлеведениеАзии. География стран, входящих в состав России или пограничных с нею, т. к. Сибири, Китайской империи, Туркестана, Независимой Татарии и Персии. – 1877. Издательство «Лань» 2014. с. 592, 636, 642.

who inhabited the region between the Hindu Kush and Suleiman mountains, and the various Indian ethnic groups dwelling between the Suleiman Mountains and the middle course of the Indus River, constituted the majority of the population of Afghanistan. At the same time, "Afghans (Pashtuns) originally lived in the Suleiman Mountains region (located in the Pakistani province of Baluchistan and the Afghan province of Zabul) and were nomadic and semi-nomadic tribes that were at a much lower level of socio-economic development."[46]

The Main Theoretical Approaches to State-Building

In general, there are three main theoretical approaches to the definitions of state-building:

The first approach (the historical approach) focuses on the historical aspects of state-building processes, from the earliest emergence of statehood to modernity. The historical approach views state-building as a complex phenomenon, which is influenced by various contributing factors such as

---

[46]Рейснер И. М. Развитие феодализма и образование государства у афганцев. – Изд-во Академии наук СССР, 1954. с. 102.

geopolitical, economic, social, cultural, ethnic, and religious. It analyzes these factors and their interrelations from a specific historical situation that is characteristic of each process of state-building. The historical approach also takes into account the relationship between internal and external factors contributing to the development. This further analyzes the relationship between different processes of state-building that coexist during the same historical period.[47] In general, the historical approach recognizes three distinctive periods, with a particular phenomenology of state-building: ancient, medieval, and modern.

In the framework of the *second approach*, state-building is viewed by some theorists as an activity undertaken by external actors (foreign countries) trying to create or restructure institutions of a weaker, post-conflict, or insolvent state. They view the state-building as an activity of a particular country concerning another.

The *third development approach* is based on a set of principles developed by the Organization for Economic Co-operation and Development in 2007

---

[47]See: Bachrach, Bernard S. *State-Building in Medieval France: Studies in Early Angevin History*. (1995). p. 59-61.

regarding support to conflict-affected states that have defined "state-building" as a field for development assistance. According to this approach, state-building is a concern within the national process based on relations between the state and society. Representatives of this viewpoint believe that countries cannot engage in state-building outside their borders; they can only influence, facilitate, support, or hinder such processes.[48]

In general, state-building is a concern as a political process based on the following components:

1) Political management (political deals);

2) Setting priorities and essential functions of the government;

3) Willingness to meet public expectations.[49]

It should be noted that experts in the field of state-building focus mainly on problems of state-building in post-conflict countries.

---

[48]Verena Fritz and Alina Rocha Menocal, *State-Building from a Political Economy Perspective: An Analytical and Conceptual Paper on Processes, Embedded Tensions and Lessons for International Engagement*, 2007; Overseas Development Institute.

[49]Whaites, Alan. *States in development: Understanding state-building: A DFID working paper*. DFID, 2008. p. 15.

The United Nations Research Institute for Social Development (UNRISD) has determined that an established state should be able to:

1) Create a stable political system and an atmosphere in which the necessary coalitions can be created, or political agreements are reached;

2) Mobilize resources for investment and social development;

3) Allocate resources between the production sector and the sector of improving the welfare of the population.[50]

With the development of this infrastructure, the state can overcome several obstacles, including the seizure of politics by influential segments of the population, opposition from interested groups, and ethnic and religious division. Developing countries tried to implement various patterns of governance and public administration developed by full democracies[51]. However, these initiatives were not

---

[50] UNRISD 2010. Building State Capacity for Poverty Reduction. Chapter 10, pp. 3–36.

[51] According to the Democracy Index compiled by the Economist Intelligence Unit (EIU), full democracies are nations where basic political freedoms and civil liberties are both respected and reinforced by the political culture. Full democracies have valid systems of checks and balances, an adequately functioning government, an independent and authoritative judiciary, and a

44

completely successful. Scholars looked back at the development of Europe to identify the key factors that helped create a bureaucracy that has been sustainable for centuries.

---

media free from infringement. (https://www.eiu.com/topic/democracy-index)

CHAPTER 2

The Historical Roots and Basics of State-building in Afghanistan

2.1. Stages of the Multi-Ethnic Statehood Formation of Modern Afghanistan

The History of the Creation of a Multi-Ethnic Afghanistan

From time immemorial, the territory of modern Afghanistan was the most important geopolitical, geo-economic, cultural and civilizational location of Asia, as the country is located in the heart of the continent and was the center of the intersection of ancient civilizations such as Ancient Persia, India, China, and Central Asia. Consequently, a colorful ethnic picture began to emerge from these times: in different periods of history, ethnic territories of representatives of Iranian, Turkic, Dard, and other ethnolinguistic groups appeared on the modern territory of Afghanistan. The Hindu Kush mountain system served as the natural boundary between the

Pashtun (Afghan) and non-Pushtun regions: in the north of the Hindu Kush, the veins are mainly Persian-speaking (Tajiks, Farsivans (Tajiks-Shiites), Hazaras, Aimaqs, etc.) and Turkic-speaking peoples (Uzbeks), and Hazaras, Charaymaks, and others), and the south was inhabited by Pashtuns (Afghans[52]).

At the beginning of the 16th century, the present territory of Afghanistan turned out to be the point of intersection of vital interests of such major regional powers as the Baburids' Empire, the State of Shaybanids (Khanate of Bukhara) and the Safavid state. Due to this, there were regular military clashes in these territories. In the 16th century, in the territory occupied by one of the East Afghan tribes – the Khattak, two feudal principalities – Akora and Teri arose. In the 17th century, another East Afghan tribe, the Afridi, formed a small feudal principality. However, these first Afghan (Pashtun) feudal principalities occupied a tiny territory and did not

---

[52]Until the 1930s, in the scientific literature and the press, the term "Afghan", "Afghan people" meant only Pashtuns. Over time, the term "Afghans" became the name of all the people of Afghanistan, regardless of their ethnicity. At the legislative level, this was reflected in the Constitutions of Afghanistan in 1964 and 1977, which declared everyone living in Afghanistan "Afghan", and the entire population of the country – "Afghan nation".

become the core of the state, which would unite within its borders all the lands inhabited by Pashtuns. The other two Afghan feudal principalities – Kandahar and Herat, which emerged in the early 18th century, did not become a nucleus. Especially a significant role of the rulers of the Ghilji principality (1709-1738) of the Hotak clan (dynasty) in the formation of the general Afghan state. Representatives of this dynasty Mir Mahmud Shah and Mir Ashraf Shah became the rulers of Persia (Safavid state) in the years 1722-1725 and 1725-1729. Nevertheless, only for the first time, the state of Durrani (1747-1819 / 1823) united all the lands inhabited by Pashtuns into a single independent state.[53] In 1751, Ahmad Shah Durrani captured the territory of Uzbeks and Tajiks on the southern bank of the Amu Darya.

The present motley ethno-confessional (including ethno-regional) map of Afghanistan and its present borders were formed during the reign of Emir Abdur Rahman Khan (1880-1901). After the final strengthening of Emir's power in Afghan Turkestan

---

[53] История Афганистана с древнейших времен до наших дней / Отв. ред. Ю. В. Ганковский. — М.: Мысль, 1982. с. 125.

(the territory on the southern coast of the Amu Darya) in 1885-1887, a borderline between the possessions of the Russian Empire and Afghanistan was established. At that time, the Pashtuns lost the overwhelming majority in the country, since the Emir ceded most of the Pashtun territories to British India by the 1893 Durand Line[54] agreement. However, at the same time, the dominance of the Pashtuns in Afghanistan has ensured thanks to the actions of Abdur Rahman Khan to centralize power, the final conquest of Hazarajat (Hazarezan) and the resettlement of Pashtuns in ethnically mixed northern regions.[55] Nevertheless, at the same time, the entire bureaucratic system carried out its work in the *Dari* language (the Afghan version of Persian-Tajik language).

To secure success, the authorities actively pursued a policy of resettlement of ethnic Pashtuns to the north of the country. In total, in the late 19th-early 20th century, 62 thousand families of ethnic Pashtuns

---

[54] Durand Line is almost untagged 2640 km border between Afghanistan and Pakistan. It arose as a result of the three Anglo-Afghan wars, in which Britain tried to expand British India. This line is the result of negotiations in 1893 between the Afghan emir Abdur Rahman Khan and the Secretary of the Indian colonial administration, Sir Mortimer Durand. The Afghan government refuses to recognize its boundary.
[55] Anwar-ul-Haq Ahady. "The decline of the Pashtuns in Afghanistan." *AsianSurvey* (1995) Vol. 35, No. 7: 621-634.

were resettled to Afghan Turkestan. One of the consequences of this was the redistribution of land ownership in favor of Pashtuns. Hence, they concentrated 10% of the best-irrigated lands in the north of Afghanistan within their hands. Mass repressions against ethnic minorities accompanied conquering campaigns in these areas. Their representatives became the primary source of replenishment of the slave trade markets. It is especially true of the Hazaras and the inhabitants of Nuristan. The hostility towards them was primarily since the Hazaras practiced Shiite Islam, and the inhabitants of Nuristan had not previously practiced Islam at all. One of the measures to suppress discontent of the non-Afghan community was their relocation towards the interiors of the country. Because of being

All these actions led to the aggravation of interethnic tension, which resulted in broad anti-government protests that acquired anti-Pashtun coloring: the revolt of the Kattagan Uzbeks (1889), Badakhshan Tajiks (1890), the movement of Aimaqs in the late 1880s, the movement in Afghan Turkestan under the leadership of Iskhak Khan, the Hazara uprising in 1892-1893 and others. Memories of the Pashtun colonization of Afghan Turkestan, the conquest of Hazarajat, the conversion of *kafir tribes* to Islam still feed the nationalist sentiments of many ethnic minorities in the country and serve as a factor in the exacerbation of ethnic-regional struggle.[56]

Features of the Ethno-Confessional Composition of Modern Afghanistan

The formation of the borders of Afghanistan, which took place under the conditions of rivalry between the British and Russian empires, led to the separation of ethnic communities. As a result, so-called divided communities (ethnic groups) prevail in Afghanistan (except for Hazaras), most of which belonged to neighboring countries (Tajikistan, Uzbekistan, Turkmenistan, Kyrgyzstan, Kazakhstan, Iran, Pakistan, India, PRC): Pashtuns, Baluch, Tajiks, Uzbeks, Kazakhs, Turkmen, Kyrgyz. This circumstance, supplemented by the isolation of

---

[56] Конфликты на Востоке: Этнические и конфессиональные: Учеб. пособие для студентов вузов / Под ред. А. Д. Воскресенского. — М.: Аспект Пресс, 2008. с. 289.

individual oases and the associated difficulties of communication, led to economic, cultural, and at times even political tensions of few ethnic groups towards neighboring countries, which caused centrifugal tendencies and cravings for foreign ethnic parts. Such happenings lead to the involvement of neighboring countries in Afghan affairs[57].

This picture is complemented by a complex of religious, linguistic, and cultural differences, which pass not only along the borders of ethnic groups but also within individual ethnic entities.

---

[57] Конфликты на Востоке: Этнические и конфессиональные: Учеб. пособие для студентов вузов / Под ред. А. Д. Воскресенского. — М.: АспектПресс, 2008. с. 289.

Chart-1. Religion in Afghanistan (percentage of the population) [58][59]

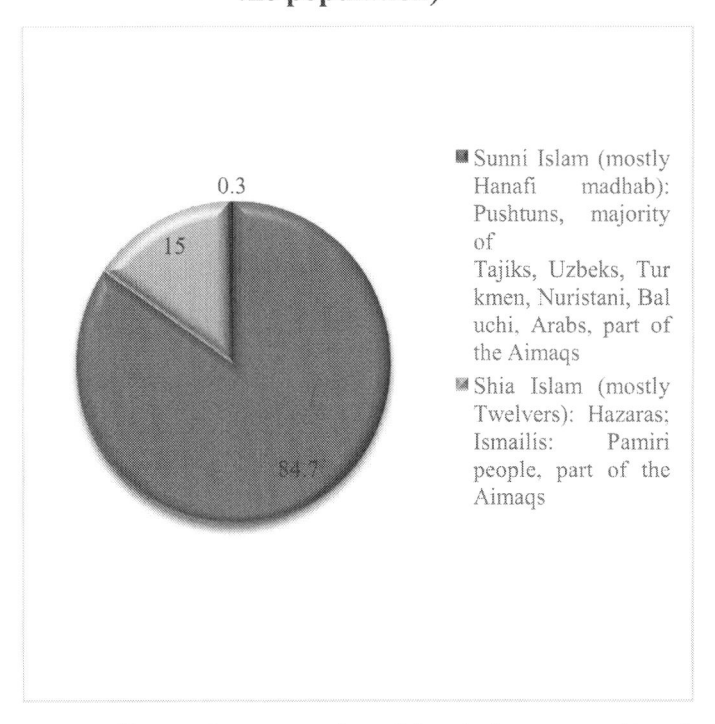

- Sunni Islam (mostly Hanafi madhab): Pushtuns, majority of Tajiks, Uzbeks, Turkmen, Nuristani, Baluchi, Arabs, part of the Aimaqs
- Shia Islam (mostly Twelvers): Hazaras; Ismailis; Pamiri people, part of the Aimaqs

(Values shown: 84.7, 15, 0.3)

Currently, more than 20 ethnic groups live in Afghanistan, and there are many ethnic and ethnographic groups. The 2004 Constitution of the Islamic Republic of Afghanistan recognized 14 ethnic groups as components of the "Afghan nation": *"The*

---

[58] World CIA Book of Facts. SouthAsia: Afghanistan. Religions. Available at: https://www.cia.gov/library/publications/the-world-factbook/geos/af.html

[59] Лалетин Ю. П. Межэтническое взаимодействие в Афганистане //Конфликты на Востоке: этнические и конфессиональные/Под ред. АД Воскресенского.–М.: Аспект Пресс. – 2008. – с. 289-314.

nation of Afghanistan shall be comprised of Pashtun, Tajik, Hazara, Uzbek, Turkman, Baluch, Pachaie (Pashai), Nuristani, Aymaq, Arab, Qirghiz, Qizilbash, Gujur (Gujjar), Brahwui, and other tribes[60]. *The word Afghan shall apply to every citizen of Afghanistan…*"[61]. Further, brief information is given on the main ethnic groups that participate in the ethno-territorial (ethnopolitical) fragmentation of the country and are interested in maintaining political influence on the power structure.

Pashtuns. Pashtuns are the most populated of all ethnic groups (there are about 14-15 million Pashtuns in the country[62]) of Afghanistan, and their number varies, according to various estimates, from 40 to 54%[63] of the population. They are concentrated mainly in the southern and eastern parts of the country. Under the genealogical traditions, the Afghan tribes were divided into four main groups (tribal

---

[60]Moghol; Pamiriethnicgroups.
[61]Constitution of the Islamic Republic of Afghanistan. Ratified January 26, 2004. Article 4.
[62]In a civil war that has been going on for almost 40 years, national censuses have not been conducted. Due to this, these figures are based on different sources. According to the World CIA Book of Facts (2018), the population of the Islamic Republic of Afghanistan as of July 2018 was 34,940,837 people.
[63]Rais, Rasul Bakhsh, and Rasul Bux Rais. *Recovering the frontier state: war, ethnicity, and state in Afghanistan.* LexingtonBooks, 2008.pp. 29-33.

confederations), by the names of the founders: *the Sarbani, the Bettani, the Gharghashti*, and *the Karlani*. The total number of tribes, according to various sources, reaches 400[64]. Durrani (Abdali) - from the Sarbani Confederation and Gilzai (Ghilji) from the Batani Confederation are the two leading tribal associations. Durrani inhabits the southern regions of Afghanistan, while Ghilji is concentrated mainly in the east of the country. The tribal structure sharply distinguishes Pashtuns from other ethnic groups (especially from Tajiks who do not have it) from Afghanistan. The Pashtuns are the world's largest ethnic group with tribal divisions. Belonging to a particular tribe plays a considerable role in intra-Pashtun relations. The council of elders and heads (*khans*) of the tribe — the *jirga* (جرگه) plays an important social and political role. Another distinctive feature of the Pashtun people is the strict observance of the rules of the unwritten code of honor - "Pashtunwali" (Pakhtunwali), which regulates almost all branches of social and everyday life of Pashtuns.

---

[64] Народы и религии мира: Энциклопедия / Гл. ред. В. А. Тишков, Редкол.: О. Ю. Артемова, С. А. Арутюнов, А. Н. Кожановский и др. — М.: Большая Российская энциклопедия, 1999. с. 63.

Tajiks. Tajiks are the second largest ethnic group after Pashtuns, and their population is about 8-9 million. Accordingly, their share in the composition of the population varies according to different sources from 20 to 33%[65]. In Afghanistan, among the Persian (meaning Tajik) settled population, there is almost no clear ethnic (national) identity and a single national ethnonym. Therefore, the ethnonym "Tajiks" (as they are called in domestic and foreign literature) refers to the sedentary, not having a tribal structure and speaking the *Dari* language (the local variant of the Persian language) known to be the population that lives mainly in the north, northeast, and west of the country. Tajiks constitute a large part of the population of such major cities as Kabul, Herat, Mazar-i-Sharif, Ghazni, and others. At the same time, they call themselves differently: *Tajiks, Farsivans* (Persian), *dehkans* (settled farmers, that is, those who do not lead a nomadic lifestyle), etc. Conventionally, the Tajik people of Afghanistan can be divided into the following groups:

---

[65] Афганистан. Население. Большая советская энциклопедия. 3-е изд. М.: «Большая советская энциклопедия». – 1970. – Т. 2. – с. 472.

This page is intentionally left blank.

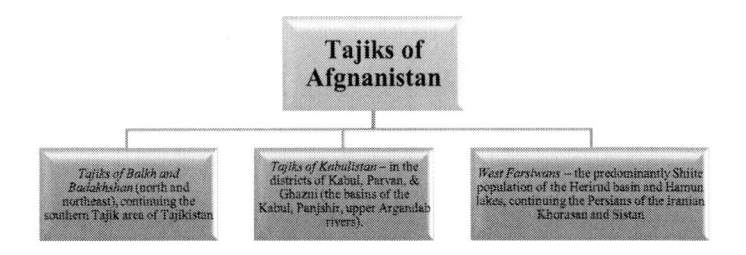

```
                    ┌─────────────────┐
                    │    Tajiks of    │
                    │   Afghanistan   │
                    └─────────────────┘
          ┌──────────────────┼──────────────────┐
┌──────────────────┐ ┌──────────────────┐ ┌──────────────────┐
│ Tajiks of Balkh and│ │Tajiks of Kabulistan│ │West Farsiwans –  │
│ Badakhshan (north  │ │– in the districts  │ │the predominantly │
│ and northeast),    │ │of Kabul, Parvan, & │ │Shiite population │
│ continuing the     │ │Ghazni (the basins  │ │of the Herirud    │
│ southern Tajik area│ │of the Kabul,       │ │basin and Hamun   │
│ of Tajikistan      │ │Panjshir, upper     │ │lakes, continuing │
│                    │ │Argandab rivers).   │ │the Persians of   │
│                    │ │                    │ │the Iranian       │
│                    │ │                    │ │Khorasan and      │
│                    │ │                    │ │Sistan            │
└──────────────────┘ └──────────────────┘ └──────────────────┘
```

Hazaras. Hazara community are an Iranian-speaking people of Turkic-Mongolian origin. Their population is nearly about 3 million, and this approximately constitutes 9%[66] of the population. Hazaras speak the ethnolect of the Dari language - *Hazaragi*, which has its borrowings from the Mongolian and Turkic languages. Mongoloid features predominate the appearance of Hazaras, and they practice Shiite Islam. Hazaras inhabit the cultural and historical area of Bamyan (Hazarajat), which is located in the heart of Afghanistan. Probably, the Hazaras are the descendants of the military settlers left by Genghis Khan in the 13th century and his successors.[67] Hazaras are the poorest and extremely marginalized of all the ethnic groups in Afghanistan. Hazaras have been

---

[66]"Afghanistan". Encyclopedia Britannica. Retrieved April 5, 2019. Available at: https://www.britannica.com/place/Afghanistan
[67]Mousavi, Sayed Askar. The Hazaras of Afghanistan. Routledge: An Historical, Cultural, Economic and Political Study, 1998. pp. 23-25.

facing discrimination for centuries mainly from the Pashtuns because of their non-Afghan origin and religious affiliation. In other words, Hazara people having Mongolian origin and being Shia Muslims had become the object of social discrimination, enslavement and military violence after the final conquer of Hazarajat and Southern Turkestan by Emir Abdur Rahman Khan. Consequently, this caused uprisings of Hazaras in 1888-1893.[68]

Uzbeks. The population of Uzbeks in Afghanistan is that of 3 million, and their share in the population is 9%[69]. They mainly dwell in the north of the country: in the provinces of Balkh, Jowzjan, Sari-Pul, Faryab, Kunduz, and the other parts of the country. The ranks of ethnic Uzbeks who historically inhabited these territories were supplemented by the flow of refugees from Turkestan after the establishment of Russian and Soviet power. They occupy a crucial geopolitical landscape between the Hindu Kush and the countries of Central Asia. Uzbeks in Afghanistan are characterized by bilingualism, that

---

[68]Hazara: History. Encyclopædia Iranica. Available at: http://www.iranicaonline.org/articles/hazara-2
[69]Hopkins, Nancy, ed. Afghanistan in 2012: A Survey of the Afghan People. Asia Foundation, 2012. p. 182

is, in addition to their native Uzbek, they are also fluent in Dari.

2.2. Drawbacks of Ethnopolitics of the Modern Afghan Government

Ethnic Confrontations in Various Stages of the Modern History of the Country

After the formation of the Durrani Empire, a definite socio-political hierarchy was formed in Afghan society, which regulated all sociopolitical processes in Afghanistan before the Saur revolution[70] (1978). According to this hierarchy, the top political authority of the country belonged exclusively to the Pashtun-Durrani, while the rest of the Pashtun tribes mostly remained outside the political establishment. Nevertheless, they constituted a privileged stratum of society. The Tajiks, being qualified personnel, held lower and medium posts in the bureaucratic system of Afghanistan. There was a large Pashtun-Tajik commercial and industrial bourgeoisie. The Uzbeks and Turkmen occupied a middle niche in the hierarchy, and among them, there were also

---

[70] The April Revolution (Saur Revolution) - the events in Afghanistan on April 27, 1978, which resulted in the establishment of a Marxist pro-Soviet government in the country.

representatives of the middle and petty bourgeoisie.[71] Although the Hazaras also had representatives of the middle and petty bourgeoisie, they still occupied the lowest part of the socio-political hierarchy.[72]

Over the half-century, there was a stable, centralized, mostly Pashtun government of King Mohammed Zahir Shah (1933-1973) in Afghanistan, which relied on foreign aid for gradual modernization. Pashtunistan[73], defined by some as an independent Pashtun state or an autonomous region in Pakistan, but viewed by others as the potentially unified state of all Pashtuns, has become a key foreign policy issue for Afghanistan. During this period, concerted efforts were made by the government to provide the rights to all citizens to establish equality between them. The relative political freedoms granted following the 1964 Constitution, allowed the formation of left-wing and Islamist groups. At the same time, ethnicity played a

---

[71] См.: *Логинов А. В.* Национальный вопрос в Афганистане // Расы и народы. М., 1990. С. 174.

[72] Rais, Rasul Bakhsh, and Rasul Bux Rais. *Recovering the frontier state: war, ethnicity, and state in Afghanistan.* Lexington Books, 2008. pp. 29-33.

[73] Pashtunistan is a modern term used to refer to a historical region populated by Pashtuns. Since the late 1940s, after the collapse of British India and the creation of Pakistan, Pashtun nationalists have periodically proposed the concept of creating an independent state of Pashtunistan.

more prominent role in political relations. "Setami Milli" (National Oppression) has become an anti-Pashtun organization, whose main goal was to overthrow what they called Pashtun domination in Afghanistan. On the other hand, "Afgan Millat" (the nationalist political party of Pashtuns) supported the great Pushtunization of Afghanistan and even sought to unite all Pashtuns. Many leaders of the two main factions (*Khalq* and *Parcham*) of the People's Democratic Party of Afghanistan (PDPA) also supported such views.[74]

The communist military coup of April 27, 1978, called the "Saur Revolution" by its instigators, marked the end of the rule of the Pashtun tribe of Durrani and opened the political arena to all the claimants. The Pashtun faction of the People's Democratic Party of Afghanistan (NDPA) Khalq tried to break the dominance of the Dari lingual culture. The regime recognized Uzbek, Turkmen, Baluchi, and Nuristan as official languages and contributed to the development of Pashtun culture. However, this policy was abolished in favor of non-Pashtun groups after the Soviet invasion in December 1979, which brought

---

[74]Abubakar Siddique, "Afghanistan's ethnic divides", Barcelona Centre for International Affairs, January 2012. p. 3.

the Parcham faction (another faction of the PDPA) to power. During the reign of the Parcham leader Babrak Karmal, Dari was promoted through Pashto, as his regime increased the presence of non-Pashtuns in the army and the state apparatus. Ethnicity also became a factor of unity and Division among the armed Islamist opposition - the *Mujahideen*[75]. In Pakistan, Pashtun Islamists firmly controlled resistance, while Iran supported the dominant groups of Hazara Shiites. In an atmosphere of internal fragmentation and external interference, President Najibullah's efforts on the intra-Afghan settlement failed. Najibullah replaced Karmal in 1986, and he had to first face the withdrawal of the Soviet army, and then the collapse of the Soviet Union. Western and regional apathy towards the country and the fierce rivalry between the mujahedeen and the communist leaders ensured that

---

[75] Afghan mojaheds are members of irregular armed formations motivated by Islamic ideology, organized into a single insurgent force during the civil war in Afghanistan in 1979-1992. Since 1979, they have been recruited from the local population in order to wage armed struggle against the Soviet military presence and the Afghan governments of Babrak Karmal and Najibullah. After the end of the war in the mid-1990s, part of the Afghan mojaheds joined the Taliban movement, and the other - the Northern Alliance units.

the UN peace plan would collapse before taking off after Najibullah left power in April 1992.[76]

The main danger for the regime of Najibullah came from the north, where there was a surge of ethnic feelings. Attempts by the Pashtuns to still dictate their conditions ran into organized resistance of ethnic minorities in the Armed Forces. Armed clashes between divisions of the 53rd and 80th infantry divisions, consisting of Uzbeks and Ismaili Shiites, on the one hand, and troops loyal to President Najibullah, on the other, have become more frequent. The commander of the 511th infantry brigade of the 53rd Division (Fayzabad, Badakhshan province), Colonel Abdul Rasul, removed the Pashtuns from posts in the provincial leadership, dismissed the commander of the 35th separate regiment of the Ministry of Internal Affairs and disarmed the regimental personnel. The commander of the 53rd Infantry Division, Colonel-General Abdul Rashid Dostum, established close contacts with the head of the Islamic Party of Afghanistan (Hezbi Islami) in the

---

[76]Siddique, Abubakar. "Afghanistan's Ethnic Divides." CIDOB Policy Research Project Sources of Tension in Afghanistan and Pakistan: A Regional Perspective. URL: http://www.observatori.org/paises/pais_87/documentos/ABUBAKAR_SIDDIQUE.pdf

province of Faryab "engineer" Nasim for joint action to expel Pashtuns from the provinces. In early 1992, Dostum established direct links with Burhanuddin Rabbani and Ahmad Shah Massoud. In February during the same year, the leaders of the northern ethnic minorities announced the formation of the "North" society and appealed to the central authorities for recognition to which Najibullah refused.[77]

The representatives of Khalq fraction Defense Minister A.Vatanjar and Air Force and Air Defense Commander General Fatah, representatives of Parcham fraction Vice President M.Rafi and others openly established contacts with Gulbuddin Hekmatyar. Even Najibullah himself tried to unite with the Pashtun forces from the opposition and searched for a compromise on a national basis. He also sought an alliance with Hekmatyar to prevent a split of Afghanistan due to the separatist sentiments of the peoples of Afghanistan, as well as the desire to preserve the dominant position of the Pashtuns in the country. On the other hand, Masoud received two influential allies surrounded by Najibullah - members

---

[77] Конфликты на Востоке: Этнические и конфессиональные: Учеб. пособие для студентов вузов / Под ред. А. Д. Воскресенского. — М.: Аспект Пресс, 2008. с. 296.

of the Politburo of the Fatherland Party, ethic Tajiks Farid Mazdak, and Daoud Kaviani. Thus, ethnonational roots turned out to be the strongest, surpassing both ideological and Islamic.[78]

In March 1992, in the province of Balkh, units of the 53rd Division took control of Mazar-i-Sharif and an airbase near it. An open speech by Dostum against Najibullah largely predetermined the fall of the regime in the last days of April. The end of the Republic of Afghanistan led to the escalation of the conflict into a phase of obvious ethnic confrontation. The strengthening of the national identity of ethnic minorities played an important role during this process.

With the advent of the Taliban movement in the political arena in 1994, the conflict gradually turned into a struggle between the Pashtun South and the non-Pashtun north. Mostly the Pashtun movement of the Taliban, using mainly the slogans of the Pashtun nationalism, during the second half of the 1990s sought to subjugate the northern regions of Afghanistan, inhabited mainly by Tajiks, Uzbeks,

---

[78] Конфликты на Востоке: Этнические и конфессиональные: Учеб. пособие для студентов вузов / Под ред. А. Д. Воскресенского. — М.: Аспект Пресс, 2008. с. 296.

Hazaras, and other non-Pushtun community. The most consistent and rigid Taliban police monitored the implementation of the imposed regulations in the cities of the northern non-Pashtun zones. The same situation was observed in the centers of several Pashtun provinces in the east of the country, where the population is predominantly Tajik, such as Ghazni, or partially Tajik, as in Khost or Jalalabad.

Moreover, the Pashtun population was squeezed out of the northern regions. Ethnic minorities did not want to go back to the times when the Pashtuns were a privileged part of the population. Additionally, the northern elite, who had full power in the territory under its control, was afraid of losing it in the event of a final victory of the Taliban.

Problems of peaceful construction in the context of ethnopolitical confrontation

After the direct intervention of foreign countries in the Afghan conflict (2001), which led to a significant change in the balance of forces in the country and the strengthening of anti-Taliban groups, the international community, and the Afghan elites faced the need to create and legitimize the government of Afghanistan.

The Bonn conference (December 2001) was devoted to solving this problem. According to the Bonn decisions, the leading state institutions, the personal composition of the temporary supreme power, were identified, and the decision was made to develop a new constitution for the country. The formation of provisional authorities preceded by the struggle of the following political groups.

Roman group. A monarchist political group that convened its congress in the fall of 2001 in Rome. Led by the former monarch Muhammad Zahir-Shah, this group was moderately liberal. Nine (9) representatives participated in the work of the Bonn conference. The Roman group, in particular, included: Abdul Sattar Sirat, Azizulla Vasifi, Hidayat Amin Arsala, Mohammad Ishaq Nadiri, Zalmai Rasul, Mohammad Amin Farhang, Mustafa Tahiri, Sima Vali, Rana Mansuri.

Northern Alliance. They are considered as the delegates of the main anti-Taliban armed forces, an alliance of warlords of the north of the country. After the death of Ahmad Shah Massoud in September

2001, he was succeeded by Mohammad Qasim Fahim. However, he and Rabbani personally did not take part in the Bonn Conference. The Northern Alliance group had a predominantly non-Pashtun character. Eleven (11) representatives of this group - in particular, Mohammad Yunus Qanuni, Dr. Abdullah Abdullah, Haji Abdul Qadir, Abas Karimi, Hussein Anvari, Mustafa Kazimi, Mohammed Natiqi, Amina Afzali, Mirvays Sadik attended in the conference was attended.

Cyprus Group. A group of pro-Iranian immigrants, which convened its founding congress in Cyprus in the same year. One of its leaders was Said Iskhak Gilani, the leader of the Afghan Sufi Tarikat Qadiriyya. Five representatives of this faction attended the conference. This group also represented the interests of the leader of the Islamic Party of Afghanistan (IPA), Hekmatyar, who was at that time in Iran. His brother-in-law Homayun Jarirah also participated in the talks.

Peshawar group. They are the Afghan Pashtun immigrants based in Pakistan. Supporters of Rasul Sayyaf led the group. He was nominally a member of the Northern Alliance but he held a more independent and radical position on several issues. Five representatives of the Sayyaf faction attended the conference.

Also, several independent field commanders and leaders of the Afghan emigration who did not join any of the listed factions took part in the conference in Bonn.[79]

The main decisions of the Bonn Conference were:
- the formation of an interim administration, which was supposed to take over the administration of Afghanistan before the formation of the transitional council;
- convocation of the Emergency Loya Jirga, which was supposed to approve the new Constitution of Afghanistan (until its approval, the Constitution of 1964 was recognized as valid except for some articles);
- the creation of a judicial system headed by the Supreme Court;

---

[79] Нессар О. «Боннская модель» и политический процесс в Афганистане в 2001–2004 гг. //Вестник Калмыцкого института гуманитарных исследований Российской академии наук. – 2016. – №. 1.

- Declaration on the need to cooperate with the international community and foreign troops stationed in the country within the framework of Security Council resolution 1386.

Conference participants met in Bonn for nine days. The subject of the most heated political debate was the question of the personal composition of the government, in particular, the election of the head of the provisional administration. Because of one of the votes, the representative of the Roman Group, Abdul Sattar Sirat, received a majority of votes as head of the provisional government. However, under US pressure, he was forced to refuse in favor of the candidacy of the then little-known Hamid Karzai. Representatives of the "Northern Alliance" insisted on their right to supreme power in the country and tried to avoid accepting the Bonn agreements. Rabbani even tried to recall the Alliance delegation from Bonn, citing her lack of authority. However, under pressure, he had to agree with the formation of a provisional administration with the participation of representatives of other groups.[80]

The Weakening of the "National Unity" Government of President Ashraf Ghani and the Strengthening of Centrifugal Forces in the North of Afghanistan in 2016-2018

The years 2016-2018 were crucial periods in the history of the presidency of Ashraf Ghani in particular, and in the process of state-building based on "ethno-confessional consent" after the collapse of the Taliban regime as a whole. Returning the leader of the Islamic Party of Afghanistan (*IPA, Hizb-e-Islam Gulbuddin*) Gulbuddin Hekmatyar to the political arena of Afghanistan after signing a peace agreement with the Government of the Islamic Republic of Afghanistan on September 29, 2016,[81] was a highly resonant event for both the political circles of

---

[80]Interviews - Dr. Abdullah Campaign Against Terror. Available at: http://www.pbs.org/wgbh/pages/frontline/shows/campaign/interviews/abdullah.html

[81] Лидер ИПА Гульбеддин Хекматъяр подписал мирный договор с правительством. 29 сентября 2016 г. [Электронный ресурс] // «Афганистан сегодня» – Информационное агентство. Режим доступа: http://www.afghanistantoday.ru/hovosti/lider-ipa-gulbeddin-hekmatyar (дата обращения: 15.04.2019).

Afghanistan and countries interested in Afghanistan. Just two years ago, the question of negotiating between official Kabul and declared by the United States to be an "international terrorist" in 2003, the "Butcher of Kabul" – Gulbuddin Hekmatyar was considered less realistic.

Such a serious step of official Kabul is due to factors emanating from the objective realities of modern Afghanistan. **First, the political establishment of Afghanistan intended to use Hekmatyar as a "mediator" in the peace negotiations between the government and the Taliban.** 2014 was a turning point in the history of Afghanistan after the fall of the Taliban regime: The International Security Assistance Force (ISAF) completed its military mission in Afghanistan, and only about 12,500 troops remained in the country.[82] After the withdrawal of the main contingent of foreign troops in 2014, the government of Afghanistan began to lose control over a significant part of the country. As of November 2016, 57.2% of the territory of

---

[82] НАТО начинает в Афганистане небоевую миссию "Решительная поддержка". 1 января 2015 г. [Электронный ресурс] // ТАСС – Информационное агентство России. Режимдоступа: http://tass.ru/mezhdunarodnaya-panorama/1682351 (датаобращения: 15.04.2019).

Afghanistan remained under the control of government forces. The territorial loss of the government compared to the same period in 2015 was 15%.[83] Besides, since January 2015, the activities of the cell of the international terrorist organization of the so-called "Islamic State" (IS) in the territory of Afghanistan have been observed.[84]

As we know, the military wing of the Hizb-e-Islami (IPA) was considered the second largest non-governmental militia after the Taliban. Consequently, the IPA's alliance with the IRA government is a "signal" for the Taliban leaders to strengthen Kabul's political power and their willingness to negotiate.

Despite the sharp contradictions between the IPA and the Taliban in the near history, they have similar goals: Hekmatyar as the Taliban opposes the presence of a foreign military contingent in Afghanistan. During his ceremonial remarks on May 4, 2017, when he arrived in Kabul after 20 years of

---

[83]Quarterly Report to the United States Congress // Special Inspector General for Afghanistan Reconstruction (SIGAR). January 30, 2017. p. 89. Available at: https://www.sigar.mil/pdf/quarterlyreports/2017-01-30qr.pdf

[84]Dearing M. Capture the Flag in Afghanistan // *Foreign Policy*. January 22, 2015. Available at: https://foreignpolicy.com/2015/01/22/capture-the-flag-in-afghanistan/

exile, he called the Taliban militants calling them "brothers" to join the peace process to "put an end to all the reasons for the presence of foreign troops" in Afghanistan. According to Hekmatyar, the leader of the Taliban opposition, Mullah Rasul, welcomed the signing of an agreement between the government and Hezb-i-Islami and did not exclude the possibility of joining the peace talks.[85]

Secondly, Ghani Intends to Consolidate His Power and Reduce the Role of Non-Pashtun Participants in the Political Arena of Afghanistan. From the very beginning of the Hizb-e-Islam armed struggle in the ranks of the Mujahidin movement against the Soviet troops, Hekmatyar showed himself as an ardent Pashtun nationalist and a supporter of radical Islam. After the overthrow of President Mohammad Najibullah and the PDPA regime, he spoke out against the election of Burhanuddin Rabbani, the ethnic Tajik president of

---

[85] Constable P. Return of warlord Hekmatyar adds to Afghan political tensions // *The Washington Post*. May 21, 2017. Available at: https://www.washingtonpost.com/world/asia_pacific/return-of-warlord-hekmatyar-adds-to-afghan-political-tensions/2017/05/18/1fa9fb20-398a-11e7-a59b-26e0451a96fd_story.html?utm_term=.22092001ffcf

the country. In this regard, Hekmatyar's views also coincide with the interests of the Taliban.

Additionally, in December 2016, one of the key players of the Afghan policy, the leader of the National Islamic Movement of Afghanistan (Jumbish), ethnic Uzbek Abdul Rashid Dostum was removed from the country's political life on charges of "kidnapping a political rival of ethnic Uzbek, the former governor of the province of Jowzjan Ahmad Eshchi, torture and rape him." Furthermore, on May 20th, 2017, it was reported that Dostum left Afghanistan and departed for Turkey.[86]

Consequently, all such events have caused a broad public and political resonance in Afghanistan, and especially among non-Pashtun political leaders. Already on June 29th, 2017, the leaders of three opposition Afghan political parties representing the interests of the **Tajik, Hazara**, and **Uzbek** groups held talks in Ankara. The negotiations were attended by the executive secretary of the Jamiat-e-Islami party (Islamic Society of Afghanistan, IOA) – former

---

[86] Срочно источник: Абдуррашид Дустум покинул Афганистан. 20 мая 2017 г. [Электронный ресурс] // «Афганистан сегодня» – Информационное агентство. Режим доступа: http://www.afghanistantoday.ru/hovosti/lider-ipa-gulbeddin-hekmatyar (дата обращения: 15.04.2019).

governor (until January 25, 2018) of Balkh Province **Atta Muhammad Nur**, second deputy head of the executive branch of the IRA, **Haji Mohammad Mohaqqiq**, who heads the Hizb Party i-Wahdat "(Party of Islamic Unity of Afghanistan, PIEA), as well as the first vice-president of the IRA, **General Abdul Rashid Dostum** - head of the party "Junbish-e-Milli"(National Islamic Movement of Afghanistan, NIDA).[87]

Following the talks, the creation of a new political alliance of these three parties, the High Council of the Coalition for the Salvation of Afghanistan, was announced. The leaders of the alliance in their draft resolution accused President Ashraf Ghani of acting outside the law and monopolizing political power.

The main requirements of the new alliance were as follows:

- make efforts to restore national harmony, maintain peace and national reconciliation process;

---

[87] В Афганистане пытаются создать «Северный альянс 2.0». 12 июля 2017 г. [Электронный ресурс] // «PolitRUS» – Экспертно-аналитическая сеть. Режим доступа: http://www.politrus.com/2017/07/12/nord-alliance/ (дата обращения: 15.04.2019).

- restore the authority of First Vice President Dostum;
- make efforts to decentralize the budget expenditures of the system in the ministries, to provide more powers to the provinces in the budget expenditures;
- make efforts to ensure balanced development and consider participation at the national level in staffing;
- conduct timely elections for the president, parliament and district councils;
- make efforts to implement security and defense reforms.[88]

On November 18th, 2017, a meeting between the First Vice-President of Afghanistan, General Abdul Rashid Dostum, and the President of Turkey, Recep Tayyip Erdogan, was held in Ankara. During the meeting with the Turkish president, the general also recalled the formation of a new political alliance

---

[88] Karim Amini. New alliance lists demands; calls for systematic reforms// The Washington Post. May 21, 2017. URL: http://www.tolonews.com/afghanistan/new-alliance-lists-demands-calls-systematic-reforms

in Afghanistan, which, he said, will play an essential role in the upcoming elections in the country.[89]

According to the director of the Center for the Study of Modern Afghanistan (CICA), Omar Nassar, "in fact, it is about an attempt to create the *Northern Alliance 2*, a political union of non-Pushtun parties. Such an attempt is connected, *firstly*, with a severe political crisis in Kabul, which began from the end of May and continues to this day, and *secondly*, with the appearance of an active player on the "Pashtun pole" in the person of Hezb-i- Islam (Islamic Party of Afghanistan) Gulbuddin Hekmatyar and, *thirdly*, with the upcoming parliamentary and presidential elections."[90]

The proximity of Hekmatyar to the political establishment of the IRA could be a catalyst for the further destabilization of Afghanistan and the collapse of the government of National Unity of President

---

[89] Абдул Рашид Дустум провел переговоры с президентом Турции. 18 ноября 2017 г. [Электронный ресурс] // «Афганистан.Ру» – Информационный портал. Режим доступа: http://afghanistan.ru/doc/116561.html (дата обращения: 15.04.2019).

[90] В Афганистане пытаются создать «Северный альянс 2.0». 12 июля 2017 г. [Электронный ресурс] // «PolitRUS» – Экспертно-аналитическая сеть. Режим доступа: http://www.politrus.com/2017/07/12/nord-alliance/ (дата обращения: 15.04.2019).

Ghani. In fact, after the signing of the peace agreement, by disbanding its militant wing, the Pashtun-oriented and extremely Islamist Hizb-e-Islam party (IPA) Hekmatyar became a counterweight to the political parties of ethnic minorities. The central part of non-Pashtun military-political leaders is extremely cautious about the decisions of President Ghani. For example, the former governor of the province of Balkh from the Jamiat-i Islami party, the ethnic Tajik Mohammed Atta Nur, assessed the situation as follows: "We welcomed the peace agreement, but instead of surrendering to the government, Mr. Hekmatyar acts as if the government had surrendered him."[91] Also, the majority of the country's non-Pashtun population, especially Kabul residents, have a negative attitude towards Hekmatyar's personality, as during the civil war (1992-1996) thousands of civilians died from his hands. Particularly, in January 1994, in an alliance with General Abdul-Rashid Dostum, he began a military confrontation with

---

[91] Constable P. Return of warlord Hekmatyar adds to Afghan political tensions // *The Washington Post*. May 21, 2017. URL: https://www.washingtonpost.com/world/asia_pacific/return-of-warlord-hekmatyar-adds-to-afghan-political-tensions/2017/05/18/1fa9fb20-398a-11e7-a59b-26e0451a96fd_story.html?utm_term=.22092001ffcf

Ahmad Shah Masoud for control of Kabul. Because of the shelling of the capital, about 4 thousand civilians died.[92]

The union of the three opposition leaders is a promising political initiative since there is a real need for a strong non-Pashtun political association on the eve of the next major electoral cycle in Afghanistan. This project is likely to be supported by various groups of Tajiks, Uzbeks, and Hazaras who are concerned about strengthening the Pashtun camp.

If the ambitions of the participants of the Northern Alliance 2 project can be kept under control, the coalition can take a large package of votes in parliamentary elections and be able to nominate a strong presidential candidate in 2019.

According to other Afghan experts, "The leaders of the three parties are too ambitious and unpredictable to be able to count on their long-term partnership seriously. There is a reason to believe that the participants in the new alliance just want to put pressure on the President of Afghanistan, Mohammad

---

[92]Gary Leupp. Meet Mr. Blowback, Gulbuddin Hekmatyar. February 14, 2003. CounterPunch.org. Available at: https://www.counterpunch.org/2003/02/14/meet-mr-blowback-gulbuddin-hekmatyar/

Ashraf Ghani, to receive personal preferences from him. As soon as Ghani satisfies some requests, for example, the same Mohaqqiq, he will leave the alliance with Nur and Dostum. We can assume that Nur also has certain personal requirements for the Arg Palace, the fulfillment of which will lead to his leaving the opposition coalition".[93]

In their opinion, most likely, the Ashraf Ghani's team will at first simply oversee the Northern Alliance 2 project, using its appearance in their interests, in particular, to continue to mobilize Pashtun politicians and voters. As the parliamentary elections approach, the Arg Palace may start splitting the opposition union, entering into separate negotiations with individual participants.

Besides, on July 2, 2018, special forces officers were arrested in the territory of Faryab province by Nizamuddin Qaysari, the chief of the Qaysar district police, and an associate of the country's first vice-president, General Abdul Rashid Dostum. In this regard, there were mass anti-

---

[93] В Афганистане пытаются создать «Северный альянс 2.0». 12 июля 2017 г. [Электронный ресурс] // «PolitRUS» – Экспертно-аналитическая сеть. Режим доступа: http://www.politrus.com/2017/07/12/nord-alliance/ (дата обращения: 15.04.2019).

government demonstrations in the north of Afghanistan, as well as significant political figures like Mohammad Mohaqiq and Atta Mohammad Nur accused the president of abuse of authority and authoritarianism.[94] Consequently, such a large-scale political reaction from the leaders of the "North" led Ghani to make certain concessions before the parliamentary elections in October 2018: on July 15, IRA President Ashraf Ghani officially stated that First Vice President General Abdul Rashid Dostum could return to Afghanistan and it is possible.[95] Consequently, on July 22, 2018, General Dostum returned to Afghanistan after 14 months of absence.

---

[94] Мохаммад Мохакик и Атта Мохаммад Нур обвинили президента в превышении полномочий. 9 июля 2018г. [Электронный ресурс] // «Афганистан.Ру» – Информационный портал. Режимдоступа: http://afghanistan.ru/doc/116561.html (датаобращения: 15.04.2019).

[95] Gen. Dostum to probably return home, says Ghani. // *Pajhwok Afghan News*. July 15, 2018. URL: https://www.pajhwok.com/en/2018/07/15/gen-dostum-probably-return-home-says-ghani

CHAPTER 3

The Prospects of the Multi-ethnic Political System in Afghanistan Through Institutional Mechanisms

3.1. External Impact on Ethnic Relations in Modern Afghanistan

As mentioned above, the formation of the borders of Afghanistan took place under the conditions of rivalry between the British and the Russian Empire, which led to the separation of ethnic communities. As a result, so-called divided communities (ethnic groups) prevail in Afghanistan (except Hazaras), most of which belonged to neighboring countries (Tajikistan, Uzbekistan, Turkmenistan, Kyrgyzstan, Kazakhstan, Iran, Pakistan, India, China): Pashtuns, Baluch, Tajiks, Uzbeks, Kazakhs, Turkmen, Kyrgyz. This circumstance, supplemented by the isolation of individual oases and the associated difficulties of communication, led to economic, cultural, and sometimes political tensions of some ethnic groups towards neighboring countries, which caused centrifugal tendencies and cravings for foreign ethnic parts. These processes lead to the involvement of neighboring countries in Afghan affairs[96].

Below, it will be individually analyzed the influence of neighboring (interested) countries on ethnic contradictions in Afghanistan:

Pakistan: The border of Afghanistan with the Islamic Republic of Pakistan is longer than the border with its other neighbors. The economy of Afghanistan is closely related to the economy of Pakistan. Since Afghanistan has the longest (2 430 kilometers) border with Pakistan, the import from this country to the Afghan economy is the largest according to the data of 2017 (USD 1.39 billion)[97]. There are also close cultural and historical ties between the two countries. Pakistan is primarily connected with Afghanistan by the presence of a significant Pashtun population on its

---

[96] Конфликты на Востоке: Этнические и конфессиональные: Учеб. пособие для студентов вузов / Под ред. А. Д. Воскресенского. — М.: АспектПресс, 2008. с. 289.
[97] Afghanistan. The Observatory of Economic Complexity by Alexander Simoes. Available at: https://oec.world/en/profile/country/afg/

territory. Today, Pashtuns are the second largest ethnic group in Pakistan after the Punjabis. Their share in the total population of the IRP is 15.42%,[98], and their population is about 30-32 million, which means in Pakistan, there are two times more Pashtuns than in Afghanistan.

Since its formation, Pakistan has developed a contradictory relationship with Afghanistan. It is primarily due to the dispute about the Durand Line: the political circles of Afghanistan, starting in 1919, began to raise the issue of the injustice of the passage of the border between Afghanistan and British India (later with Pakistan) and actively supported the idea of creating Pushtunistan (a country uniting the ethnic territory of all Pashtuns). Consequently, in this regard, Afghan politicians had differences with the leadership of Pakistan. On the other hand, the Pashtuns also had a significant influence in the political circles of Pakistan and naturally, in a certain sense, supported the Pashtun power in neighboring Afghanistan. Presidents of Pakistan Ayub Khan (1958-1969), Yahya Khan (1969-1971) and Ghulam Ishaq Khan

---

[98]Taus-Bolstad, Stacy. *Pakistan in Pictures*. Visual geography series (Revised ed.). Minneapolis: Twenty-First Century Books, 2003.. p. 41.

(1988-1993), Prime Minister Imran Khan (2018-presently), Chairman of the Senate (the upper house of the Parliament of Pakistan) Habibullah Khan (1973-1977), as well as the Speaker of the National Assembly (the lower house of the Parliament of Pakistan) Gohar Ayub Khan (1990-1993), are ethnic Pashtuns.[99]

In the time of the Afghan war (1979-1989), Pakistan placed camps and headquarters of the Mujahidin movement on its territory, and actively supported the military-political leaders of the Pashtuns. Also, due to disagreements with the Rabbani government, Pakistan's Inter-Services Intelligence (ISI) began to actively support the pro-Pushtun movement of the Taliban until September 11th, 2001. Official Islamabad is also often accused of encouraging hostile relations between Pashtuns and other ethnic groups, as well as using the multi-ethnic nature of Afghan society in their strategic interests.

In general, the policy of Islamabad is aimed at establishing control over the central government of Afghanistan through Pashtun leaders who support the

---

[99] Aziz, Sartaj. *Between Dreams and Realities: Some Milestones in Pakistan's History*. Karachi, Pakistan: Oxford University Press, 2009. p. 408.

conservative Islamic views and policies of Pakistan. The main reasons for this foreign policy are, **firstly**, to ensure the territorial integrity of the country and remove from the agenda the issue of the Durand Line, and **secondly**, to use the territory of Afghanistan as a "strategic depth" in cases of military conflict with India.[100] Since, due to the relatively narrow length of Pakistan's territory from east to west (about 600-700 km in total) from military strategy, Pakistan is forced to find strategic depth in cases of large-scale military conflict with India.

Iran: Iran's intervention in ethnic relations in Afghanistan is due to the presence of a Shiite minority in Afghanistan, approximately 20% of the country's population. Most of the Shiites in Afghanistan are the Twelver's. Few of them are Ismaili Shiites.[101] The Afghan war served as the beginning of the open support of the Shiites of Afghanistan from the Islamic Republic of Afghanistan (1979-1989). It was during

---

[100]Weinbaum, Marvin G. "Afghanistan and its Neighbors, An Ever Dangerous Neighborhood" *Special Report* 162 (2006): 12. Available at: https://www.usip.org/sites/default/files/sr162.pdf
[101]Michael V. Bhatia; Mark Sedra. *Afghanistan, Arms and Conflict: Armed Groups, Disarmament and Security in a Post-War Society*. Psychology Press, 2008. pp. 252

these years that a coalition of the Shiite parties of the Mujahidin movement – the Shiite Eight (Tehran Eight) was formed in Iran.[102]

Besides, Iran seeks to prevent the resurgence of a radical Sunni regime in Afghanistan, be it the Taliban or similar groups. Tehran is especially wary of the spread of Saudi-sponsored Wahhabism in Afghanistan. Iran considers itself the patron saint of its co-religionists in Afghanistan and mainly ethnic Hazara.[103] Although Tehran's relations with Afghan Shiite political parties and militias were not always close, it always favored a multi-ethnic Afghan government.

Central Asian countries: Despite the historical, cultural, and ethnic proximity of the Central Asian republics (primarily Tajikistan and Uzbekistan) to Afghanistan, they see Afghanistan primarily in the security context. Especially Tajikistan had particular concerns about radical Tajik groups in Afghanistan

---

[102]Ruttig, T. *Islamists, Leftists — and a Void in the Center. Afghanistan's Political Parties and where they come from (1902—2006).* Available at: http://www.kas.de/wf/doc/kas_9674-544-2-30.pdf

[103]Weinbaum, Marvin G. "Afghanistan and its Neighbors, An Ever Dangerous Neighborhood" *Special Report* 162 (2006): 12. Available at: https://www.usip.org/sites/default/files/sr162.pdf

who participated in the civil war in Tajikistan. However, in recent times there has been some action by these countries aimed at ethnic Uzbeks and Tajiks living in northern Afghanistan. For instance, the opening of an Educational center for training Afghan citizens at the Ministry of Higher and Secondary Special Education of the Republic of Uzbekistan on January 23rd, 2018, in the Termez region of Uzbekistan reflects the country's attempts to conduct "soft power."

In turn, such countries as **China** and **India** are also interested in the political stabilization of Afghanistan. Afghanistan from the base of radical groups is also a threat to them. China fears that the territory of Afghanistan has not become a center of Uyghur resistance. At the same time, India is also not interested in the fact that there were terrorist organizations on the territory of Afghanistan that might act against India.

3.2. Democratic Institutions and Prospects for Promoting the Mutual Interests of Ethnic Groups in Modern Afghanistan

Undoubtedly, one of the leading causes of instability in Afghanistan is the weakness of the country's political system, civil society institutions, and other democratic mechanisms of state-building. As the historical experience of emerging democracies shows, in the absence of stability of the political establishment (political system), the fragmentation potential increases.[104] In this section, I would like to analyze the main shortcomings of the current political system of Afghanistan, as well as democratic institutions and prospects for advancing the mutual interests of ethnic groups in modern Afghanistan. Furthermore, it is also to formulate particular suggestions (models) on improving the political system of Afghanistan.

---

[104] Mansfield, Edward D., and Jack Snyder. "Democratization and war." *Foreign Affairs*. 74 (1995): p. 79.

Presidency Institute in Afghanistan

As mentioned above, the ethno-national confrontation primarily affected the process of adopting the new Constitution of Afghanistan (2004), which determined its difficulties and drama. In particular, the proposed version of the presidential republic met with opposition from representatives of ethnic minorities who defended the *parliamentary form of government* and did not want to concentrate power in the hands of the president – Pashtun. It was around this issue that the main controversy flared up. Burhanuddin Rabbani headed the opposition. Hamid Karzai threatened that he would not run for president unless the Jirga approved the presidential form of government.[105] The result of the bargaining was a compromise on which Afghanistan remained a presidential republic, but the powers of the president were curtailed; he cannot dissolve the parliament. The lower house must approve the proposed government.

---

[105] Лалетин Ю. П. Межэтническое взаимодействие в Афганистане //Конфликты на Востоке: этнические и конфессиональные/Под ред. АД Воскресенского.–М.: Аспект Пресс. – 2008. – с. 289-314.

However, the parliament does not have the right to impeach the president.[106][107]

In this regard, the main point of contention is the excessive powers of the President of Afghanistan. The fact that the president has the constitutional authority to appoint officials down to the district level[108] makes him not only the head of state but also the only *decision-maker* in the political system of Afghanistan. Consequently, this contradicts not only the democratic principle of "separation of powers" but also the interests of other political (ethnopolitical) forces of Afghanistan. According to Samuel Huntington, "the ability to create political institutions is the ability to create public interests."[109]

Political Parties

As we know, political parties rationally distribute the inevitable political differences that exist

---

[106] Rubin, Barnett R. "Crafting a constitution for Afghanistan." *Journal of Democracy* 15.3 (2004): 5-19.

[107] See: Constitution of the Islamic Republic of Afghanistan. Ratified January 26, 2004. Chapter Three: The President (11 articles), Chapter Five: National Assembly (29 articles).

[108] Smith, Scott. "The Future of Afghan Democracy." *Stability: International Journal of Security and Development* 3.1: 12 (2014) pp. 1-9.

[109] Huntington, Samuel P. *Political order in changing societies*. Yale University Press, 2006. p. 24.

in any political community. The post-Bonn political system in Afghanistan, where the president of the country is an ethnic Pashtun, has "infinite power" and there is a "weak" parliament encouraged creation of ethnopolitical parties as well as the consolidation of political forces based on ethno-confessional interests. In turn, the country's president wants to act as a symbol (embodiment) of national unity, but many political parties are the driving force for the decentralization of power.[110]

At this early stage of Afghan political modernization and democratization, *ethnic groups are also interest groups. Ethnic solidarity* is often the most reliable sign of political trust and identity. Today, there are more than 80 political parties in Afghanistan. *Table 2* gives detailed information on the aims (ideology) of the political parties in Afghanistan, presented in the lower house of parliament of Afghanistan following the 2010 parliamentary elections. Analyzing the data provided in the table, it is possible to reveal how deeply ethno-

---

[110]Smith, Scott. "The Future of Afghan Democracy." *Stability: International Journal of Security and Development* 3.1: 12 (2014) pp. 1-9.

confessional interests intervened in the political arena of Afghanistan.

Table 2. Political Parties of Afghanistan, Represented in the Lower House (House of the People) of the Parliament of Afghanistan (National Assembly) Based on the 2010 Parliamentary Elections[111]

No.	Party name	Leader	Ideology	Seats in the lower house
1.	Islamic Society of Afghanistan (Jamiat-e Islami)	Salahuddin Rabbani	Islamism, Communitarism, Tajik interests	17
2.	People's Islamic Unity Party of Afghanistan (PIUPA)	Mohammad Mohaqiq	Hazara nationalism	11
3.	National Islamic Movement of Afghanistan (Junbish)	Abdul Rashid Dostum	Uzbek interests, Turkmen interests, Secularism	10
4.	Republican Party of Afghanistan	Sebghatullah Sanjar	Human rights, Social liberalism, Secularism, Feminism, Egalitarianism	9
5.	Islamic Unity	Karim	Hazara	7

[111] Based on materials from the official website of the House of the People (Wolesi Jirga) of the National Assembly of the Islamic Republic of Afghanistan. Available at: http://wj.parliament.af/

	Party of Afghanistan (Hezbe Wahdat)	Khalili	minority rights, Shia Islamism	
6.	National Islamic Front of Afghanistan	Ahmed Gailani	Pashtun nationalism, Pashtun interests	6
7.	Afghan Social Democratic Party (Afghan Millat)	Stanagul Sherzad	Pashtun nationalism, Social democracy	4
8.	Islamic Dawah Organisation of Afghanistan	Abdul Rasul Sayyaf	Pashtun and Tajik interests, Islamism	4
9.	Islamic Movement of Afghanistan	Said Mohammad Ali Jawid	Shia Islamism	4
10.	National Solidarity Party of Afghanistan	Sayed Mansur Naderi	Ismaili Shia interests	4
11.	Islamic Party of Afghanistan (Hezbi Islami)	Gulbuddin Hekmatyar	Islamism, Pashtun interests	1
12.	National Islamic Unity Party of Afghanistan	Muhammad Akbari	Shia Islamism, Hazara minority rights, Religious conservatism	1
13.	National Movement of Afghanistan	-	-	1
14.	National Solidarity Movement of Afghanistan	Sayed Is'haq Gailani	Monarchism	1

15.	National Sovereignty	-	-	1
16.	National United Party of Afghanistan	Nur ul-Haq Ulumi	Secularism, Progressivism, Socialism, Feminism	1
17.	New Afghanistan Party (Naveen)	Yunus Qanuni	-	1
18.	People's Islamist Movement	-	-	1
Total seats in the lower house				**84**[112]
OTHER INFLUENTIAL POLITICAL PARTIES				
19.	National Coalition of Afghanistan	Abdullah Abdullah	Sectarianism, Islamism, Populism	
20.	Truth and Justice Party	Hanif Atmar	Multi-ethnic, Reformism, Eurasianism	
21.	National Congress Party of Afghanistan	Abdul Latif Pedram	Secularism, Liberalism	

Administrative division of Afghanistan: Another obstacle to the centralization of official Kabul's power is the presence of an extensive (in a certain sense, excessive) number of administrative divisions of the first level. If from 1929 to 1963 there were only

---

[112] Of the 249 members of the lower chamber, 165 are independent (non-partisan) politicians. Based on materials from the official website of the House of the People (Wolesi Jirga) of the National Assembly of the Islamic Republic of Afghanistan. Available at: http://wj.parliament.af/

nine provinces in Afghanistan[113], today Afghanistan is administratively divided into 34 provinces (*wilayat* - ولایت), they, in turn, are divided into 398 districts (*wuleswali* - ولسوالی). In this case, the total territory of the country is 652,230 square kilometers, and the population is 34,940,837 people (July 2018).[114] Consequently, this complicates the management process, increases the expenditures, encourages red tape and corruption. Since an extended number of divisions, require additional expenditures for administrative officials and bureaucracy. Furthermore, it is too difficult to control these officials in terms of preventing corruption. Below a comparative analysis of the administrative division of several countries in Africa, Asia, and Europe will be given, which are close to Afghanistan in terms of area and population:

---

[113]Mukhopadhyay, Dipali. *Warlords, strongman governors, and the state in Afghanistan.* Cambridge University Press, 2014. p. 43.
[114]Afghanistan. The World Factbook. Central Intelligence Agency. The United States. Available at: https://www.cia.gov/library/publications/the-world-factbook/geos/af.html

Table 3. Comparative Analysis of the First-Order (First-Level) Administrative Divisions of Some Countries of Africa, Asia, and Europe[115]

No.	Country	Population (July 2018)	Total area in km²	Number of first-level divisions	The average population of divisions
1.	Malaysia	31 809 660	329 847	17	1 900 000
2.	Morocco	34 314 130	446 550	12	2 800 000
3.	Poland	38 420 687	312 685	16	2 400 000
4.	Saudi Arabia	33 091 113	2 149 690	13	2 000 000
5.	Uzbekistan	33 375 800	448 900	14	2 400 000
AVERAGE:		*34 200 000*	*737 500*	*14*	*2 300 000*

There are different approaches to the essence of ethnic conflict regulations in contemporary social sciences. For instance, McGarry and O'Leary present several macro-methods of ethnic conflict regulation. Consequently, *consociationalism (power-sharing)* and *federalization* are considered relatively acceptable

---

[115] Based on materials from the World Factbook. Central Intelligence Agency. United States. Available at: https://www.cia.gov/library/publications/the-world-factbook/

forms of management in terms of Afghanistan.[116] Since, there are several large ethnic groups ("divided nations"), which share the common Afghan territory. Consequently, these forms might maintain the territorial integrity of Afghanistan and the consolidation of all ethnic-confessional groups into the united Afghan nation.

Based on the above considerations, the following proposals (models) for improving the political system of Afghanistan, strengthening the foundations of statehood and promoting the peace process can be identified:

1. Regarding the Form (System) of Government of the Islamic Republic of Afghanistan

As above-mentioned, the institution of the presidency in Afghanistan has become the central object of political debate and controversy. Also, the extensive powers of the president only aggravate the inter-Afghan conflict between the country's main military-political forces.

---

[116]McGarry, John, and Brendan O'leary, eds. *The politics of ethnic conflict regulation: Case studies of protracted ethnic conflicts*. Routledge, 2013. pp. 30-37.

In this regard, one of the ways to resolve these differences is the transition to a *parliamentary* or *semi-presidential* form of government. The interests of all the ethnopolitical forces of Afghanistan can be represented only in a professional and robust parliament, based on the principle of the legitimate rule of the majority and respect for the rights of minorities. Additionally, the post of *Prime Minister (Chief Executive)* should be enshrined in the country's Constitution. Since in such systems the political interests of each large ethnic group might be represented proportionally. Furthermore, the post of Prime Minister, which should be appointed by the parliament can maintain the system of "checks and balances" in the Afghan government and prevent the abuse of political power by the President.

As we know, according to the Bonn agreements, Pashtuns were given 33%, Tajiks 24.5%, Hazaras 19%, and Uzbeks 13% of the seats in the government of post-Taliban Afghanistan.[117] However,

---

[117] Лалетин Ю. П. Межэтническое взаимодействие в Афганистане //Конфликты на Востоке: этнические и конфессиональные/Под ред. АДВоскресенского. – М.: АспектПресс. – 2008. – с. 289-314.

these proportions were not followed since the President became completely independent. Consequently, this also contributed to the destabilization of the situation in the country. In this regard, it would be appropriate to consider the issue of limiting the powers of the President, as well as the quota system on an ethnic-confessional basis in the legislative and executive authorities of Afghanistan. However, these reforms can cause displeasure from Pashtun nationalists.

2. Reforms should be carried out regarding the Form of Territorial Structure and the Administrative Division of Afghanistan

The issue of the federalization of the country appeared on the agenda after the overthrow of the Najibullah regime and the declaration of the Islamic State of Afghanistan in 1992. There was a crucial role of ardent supporters of the military-political leaders of the Uzbeks (General Dostum) and Hazaras in this process. However, this model has not gained popularity among politicians, Pashtuns, and Tajiks. Consequently, it was not mentioned in the Bonn

Agreement. Nevertheless, the federalization of Afghanistan remains one of the controversial issues of the country's political system.

Firstly, in modern political history, the federalization of a country is considered one of the possible ways to resolve the inter-ethnic conflict in post-conflict states. For example, the civil war in Ethiopia (1974-1991) and the Bosnian war (1992-1995) was settled through the federalization. In the case of Bosnia and Herzegovina, the country divided into two de facto independent entities of each federation – the Federation of Bosnia and Herzegovina and the Republika Srpska (Serb Republic). Their executive, legislative, and judicial bodies operate independently of each other. To carry out state functions at the federal level, a collective supreme body of executive power – the Presidency of Bosnia and Herzegovina were created. The Presidium consists of three members elected at the same time for four years, one from each constituent ethnic groups (*Bosniaks (Bosnian Muslims), Serbs* and *Croats*). The President (Chairman) of the Presidency is elected of the three members of the Presidency, followed by a rotation every eight months, which ensures equality of nationalities. The Presidency implements foreign and financial policies, as well as performs representative functions.[118] However, at the same time, the subjects (entities) of the federation do not have the right to leave the federation. Today, the case of Bosnia is considered as a classic model of a *decentralized federation*.

Secondly, the Pakistani model of a *centralized federation* that is more or less stable in the neighboring country of Afghanistan may be acceptable for Afghanistan. Pakistan is divided into four provinces, one federal capital territory and two territories of Kashmir, administratively subordinate to Pakistan.[119] Four central provinces were established in the ethnic territory of the four main ethnic groups of Pakistan (*Punjabis, Pashtuns, Sindhi*, and *Baluch*), which is in the political interests of the country's main ethnopolitical forces. A parliamentary majority in the Provincial Assembly elects the Chief Ministers (Chief Executives) of the provinces. At that time, the

---

[118]See: Dayton agreement - UN Peacemaker - the United Nations. December 14, 1995. Available at: https://peacemaker.un.org/sites/peacemaker.un.org/files/BA_951121_DaytonAgreement.pdf

[119]See: Constitution of the Islamic Republic of Pakistan. Ratified August 14, 1973.

President of Pakistan, at the suggestion of the Prime Minister, appoints Governors (nominal and ceremonial heads) of provinces.[120] The past years have shown the relative stability of the federal structure of Pakistan.

Nevertheless, it should be noted that the federalization of Afghanistan unambiguously causes an adverse reaction at the same time from the Pashtun nationalists and external actors (primarily Pakistan and Tajikistan), who fear increased separatist sentiments amongst their people. However, as already noted, the current administrative division of Afghanistan does not correspond to the current realities. It should be revised (that is, the number of first-level administrative units should be reduced by an average of 14 units. *See Table 3*) based on the experience of other countries.

3. The Future Government of Afghanistan must remain Islamic

Since the beginning of the Afghan war (1979), Islam became the unifying factor of the political and

---
[120] Ibid

armed opposition. First against the Soviet troops, and then in the process of the formation of a new Afghan state. At the present stage, when there is a desire of the government of Afghanistan to conclude a peace treaty with the Taliban and subsequently provide them with seats in the government, the preservation of the Islamic identity of the country's political system is the guarantor of the stabilization of the political situation. The importance of this factor was highlighted by the US Special Representative for Afghanistan Reconciliation, Zalmay Khalilzad, following the next round of talks (February-March, 2019) with the Taliban in Doha, saying that the United States agrees that the future Afghan government will be Islamic.[121]

However, the fundamental principles of democracy (*freedom of speech, people's power, the elected head of state, ensuring equality and justice in government*, etc.) do not contradict Islamic beliefs. Instead, they have the same standard features in many

---

[121]Mujib Mashal. 2 Weeks of U.S.-Taliban Talks End with "Progress" but No Breakthrough. *The New York Times*. March 12, 2019. Available at: https://www.nytimes.com/2019/03/12/world/asia/afghanistan-us-taliban-talks.html

aspects.[122] Most Muslim scholars believe that the democratic process is similar to the early Islamic era (the era of the Rashidun Caliphate) when people elected their leaders through councils (*Shuras*) in the form of direct elections. In this regard, Islamic values are compatible with liberal and democratic ideals.

---

[122] de Zeeuw, Jeroen, and Krishna Kumar, eds. *Promoting democracy in postconflict societies*. Boulder, CO: LynneRienner, 2006.

CONCLUSION

Considering the relationship of ethnic groups in Afghanistan allows us to conclude that the national question now constitutes the central nerve of the country's public and political life and also affects all spheres of social activities. Ethnic tensions influence political processes. The latter is caused by the reluctance of consolidated ethnic minorities, led by an influential elite, to abandon their positions. On one hand, and Pashtun's discontent with a too large representation of ethnic minorities, and especially Tajiks, in central authorities and the desire to restore Pashtun dominance - on the other. All this testifies to the fact that ethnonational contradictions in Afghan society are profound and affect the very foundations of government.

At the same time, in the medium and long term, positive developments cannot be ruled out. They can provide the effect of restoring the economy after a devastating war. This kind of effect was observed in many countries at the stage of exiting world and civil wars, both in the twentieth century and in earlier eras. At the same time, the assertion of a stable statehood of both democratic and authoritarian category usually became the main conditions for growth. From the prospects of strengthening Afghanistan as a single centralized state, beyond any doubt, it depends on the implementation of favorable scenarios for its development. In other words, the key to solving social and economic problems lies in the political sphere, and various other respects depend on the quality of the leaders, their ability to rise above localist and egoistic interests. Success in the political field also depends on the quality of decisions made.

The complexity of solving the problems facing the Afghan society places unique demands on the quality of the Afghan political elite and also implies a reliable partnership of Afghanistan with interested international organizations and states. It is evident that without such a partnership, the leading national state-political tasks that constitute the substantive part of the Afghan political process cannot be solved.

It can be concluded that **without the efforts of the leading political forces of Afghanistan, which represent the interests of the main ethnic and religious groups of the country**, it is impossible to carry out the process of national reconciliation in

Afghanistan. In turn, this postulate was also reflected at the international conference on Afghanistan: "Peace Process, Security Cooperation, and Regional Cooperation," which was held on March 27th, 2018, in Tashkent.

In this regard, it would be appropriate to present the forecast of the leading Russian specialists on Afghanistan on the prospects of ethnopolitical contradictions in Afghanistan. After analyzing various kinds of expert materials, Belokrenitsky and Sikoev identify three main scenarios[123]:

1. The first one is favorable for the current regime and international security. It involves strengthening the position of the current government in Kabul within the country, in the global and regional arenas. The scenario assumes the preservation of the system for the distribution of command roles between President Ghani and the head of the executive branch (Abdullah Abdullah) and the establishment of constructive interaction between the legislative and executive branches of government. Strengthening the regime will be facilitated by the accession to the

---

[123] Белокреницкий В. Я., Сикоев Р. Р. Движение Талибан и перспективы Афганистана и Пакистана //Москва, ИВ РАН. – 2014. с. 189-198.

reconciliation process of a new group of Taliban leaders.

2. *The second scenario* is unfavorable – which is the return of the Taliban to power.

3. The third scenario is too unfavorable, factual disintegration of the country, the Talibanization of the south and east of Afghanistan and northwest Pakistan. The situation in this scenario will return to the mid-1990s. The task of the Taliban will be to control not only over Jalalabad, Kandahar, and Kabul but also the subordination of the west, center, and north. The intermediate variant is the actual split, fragmentation of the country with the formation of the Taliban enclaves of power ("Islamist principalities") in the south and east of the country, the separation of the Iranian influence of the western region (Herat), and fully independent north ("Uzbek emirate") and the northeast Tajik enclave with its center in Panjshir.

BIBLIOGRAPHY

I. Legal Documents:

1. Agreement on Provisional Arrangements in Afghanistan Pending the Re-establishment of Permanent Government Institutions (Bonn Agreement). December 12, 2001.

2. Declaration of the Tashkent Conference on Afghanistan: Peace Process, Security Cooperation, and Regional Connectivity (Tashkent Declaration). Tashkent, Republic of Uzbekistan. March 26-27, 2018.

3. Constitution of the Islamic Republic of Afghanistan. Ratified January 26, 2004.

4. Constitution of the Islamic Republic of Pakistan. Ratified August 14, 1973.

5. General Framework Agreement for Peace in Bosnia and Herzegovina (Dayton Agreement). November 21, 1995.

II. Academic Monographs and other Scholarly Literature in English:

6. Adeney, Katharine. *Federalism and ethnic conflict regulation in India and Pakistan.* Springer, 2016.

7. Anderson, Benedict. *Imagined communities: Reflections on the origin and spread of nationalism*. VersoBooks, 2006.

8. Ahmed, Faiz. *Afghanistan Rising: Islamic Law and Statecraft Between the Ottoman and British Empires*. HarvardUniversityPress, 2017.

9. Aziz, Sartaj. *Between Dreams and Realities: Some Milestones in Pakistan's History*. Karachi, Pakistan: Oxford University Press, 2009.

10. Bachrach, Bernard S. *State-Building in Medieval France: Studies in Early Angevin History*. (1995).

11. Caplan, Richard, ed. *Exit strategies and state-building*. Oxford University Press, 2012.

12. Chomsky, Noam. *Failed states: The abuse of power and the assault on democracy*. Metropolitan Books, 2007.

13. Ghani, Ashraf, and Clare Lockhart. *Fixing failed states: A framework for rebuilding a fractured world*. Oxford University Press, 2009.

14. Guelke, Adrian, ed. *Democracy and ethnic conflict: advancing peace in deeply divided societies*. Springer, 2004.

15. Huntington, Samuel P. *Political order in changing societies.* Yale University Press, 2006.

16. Jackson, Robert H. *Quasi-states: sovereignty, international relations, and the Third World.* Vol. 12. Cambridge University Press, 1993.

17. Lee, Jonathan L. *Afghanistan: A History from 1260 to the Present.* Reaktion Books, 2018.

18. McGarry, John, and Brendan O'leary, eds. *The politics of ethnic conflict regulation: Case studies of protracted ethnic conflicts.* Routledge, 2013.

19. Michael V. Bhatia; Mark Sedra. *Afghanistan, Arms, and Conflict: Armed Groups, Disarmament, and Security in a Post-War Society.* Psychology Press, 2008.

20. Mukhopadhyay, Dipali. *Warlords, strongman governors, and the state in Afghanistan.* CambridgeUniversityPress, 2014.

21. People, James; Bailey, Garrick (2010). *Humanity: An Introduction to Cultural Anthropology* (9th ed.). Wadsworth Cengage learning.

22. Rais, Rasul Bakhsh, and Rasul Bux Rais. *Recovering the frontier state: war, ethnicity, and state in Afghanistan.* Lexington Books, 2008.

23. Roselle, Laura. *Research and writing in international relations.* Routledge, 2016.

24. Rotberg, Robert I., ed. *When states fail: causes and consequences.* Princeton University Press, 2010.

25. Shoup, Brian. *Conflict and cooperation in multi-ethnic states: institutional incentives, myths, and counter-balancing.* Routledge, 2007.

26. Taus-Bolstad, Stacy. *Pakistan in Pictures.* Visual geography series (Revised ed.). Minneapolis: Twenty-First Century Books, 2003.

27. Verena Fritz and Alina Rocha Menocal, *State-Building from a Political Economy Perspective: An Analytical and Conceptual Paper on Processes, Embedded Tensions, and Lessons for International Engagement,* 2007; Overseas Development Institute.

28. Whaites, Alan. *States in development: Understanding state-building: A DFID working paper.* DFID, 2008.

29. Zartman, I. William, ed. *Collapsed states: the disintegration and restoration of legitimate authority*. Lynne Rienner Publishers, 1995.

30. de Zeeuw, Jeroen, and Krishna Kumar, eds. *Promoting democracy in postconflict societies*. Boulder, CO: Lynne Rienner, 2006.

III. Academic Monographs and other Scholarly Literature in Russian:

31. Афганистан в начале XXI века. Институт востоковедения РАН. Ответственный редактор: В.Коргун. М., 2004.

32. Белокреницкий В. Я., Сикоев Р. Р. Движение Талибан и перспективы Афганистана и Пакистана //Москва, ИВ РАН. – 2014.

33. Вебер, Макс. Политика как призвание и профессия. *Избранные произведения* (1990): 644-706.

34. Во имя мира, стабильности и прогресса. Материалы международной конференции высокого уровня по Афганистану «Мирный процесс, сотрудничество в сфере безопасности и региональное взаимодействие». Ташкент. 27 марта 2018 года.

35. История Афганистана с древнейших времен до наших дней / Отв. ред. Ю. В. Ганковский. — М.: Мысль, 1982.

36. Каутский К. О материалистическом понимании истории. – Основа, 1923.

37. Конфликты на Востоке: Этнические и конфессиональные: Учеб. пособие для студентов вузов / Под ред. А. Д. Воскресенского. — М.: Аспект Пресс, 2008.

38. Народы и религии мира: Энциклопедия / Гл. ред. В. А. Тишков, Редкол.: О. Ю. Артемова, С. А. Арутюнов, А. Н. Кожановский и др. — М.: Большая Российская энциклопедия, 1999.

39. Рейснер И. М. Развитие феодализма и образование государства у афганцев. – Изд-во Академии наук СССР, 1954.

40. Риттер К. Землеведение Азии. География стран, входящих в состав России или пограничных с нею, т. к. Сибири, Китайской империи, Туркестана, Независимой Татарии и Персии. – 1877. Издательство «Лань» 2014.

41. Сорокин П. А., Согомонов А. Ю. Человек, цивилизация, общество. – Издательство политической литературы, 1992.

42. Туляганова Н.У. Афганский фактор в современных международных отношениях в Центральной Азии. Ташкент: Фан, 2004.

43. Умаров А.А. Афганистан и региональная безопасность Центральной Азии: начало XXI века: Монография, – Ташкент, УМЭД 2017.

44. Файзуллаев А., Аллисон Р. (отв, ред,), Предотвращение региональных конфликтов и содействие стабильности в Центральной Азии и Афганистане: Материалы Международной конференции (22-23 ноября 2004 г., Ташкент, Узбекистан). – Ташкент: УМЭД 2005.

45. Хасанов У.А. Региональная безопасность и национальные интересы (Центральноазиатский регион). – М.: Вагриус, 2004.

46. «Этнический конфликт: теория, экспертиза, пути решения». Сборник «Школа миротворческих инициатив» / Составители:

М.А.Юндина, В.А.Авксентьев, С.А.Рубашкина, А.В.Зотова. Ставрополь: 2001.

47. Ядов, В. А. Социологическое исследование: методология, программа, методы. Самара, 1995.

48. Язык и этнический конфликт / Под ред. М. Брилл Олкотт и И. Семенова; Моск. Центр Карнеги. — М.: Гендальф, 2001. – 150 с.

IV. Scholarly Articles in English:

49. Abdulloev, Rakhmatullo. "Influence of the ethnic factor on the formation of Afghan statehood." *Central Asia & the Caucasus (14046091)* 15.1 (2014).

50. Anwar-ul-Haq Ahady. "The decline of the Pashtuns in Afghanistan." *AsianSurvey* (1995) Vol. 35, No. 7: 621-634.

51. Call, Charles T. "Beyond the 'failed state': Toward conceptual alternatives." *European Journal of International Relations* 17.2 (2011): 303-326.

52. Call, Charles T. "Building states to build peace? A critical analysis." *Journal of Peacebuilding & Development* 4.2 (2008): 60-74.

53. Eriksen, Stein Sundstøl. "'State failure' in theory and practice: the idea of the state and the contradictions of state formation." *Review of International Studies* 37.1 (2011): 229-247.

54. Gordon, Ruth. "Saving failed states: sometimes a neocolonialist notion." *Proceedings of the ASIL Annual Meeting*. Vol. 91. Cambridge University Press, 1997.

55. Helman, Gerald B., and Steven R. Ratner. "Saving failed states." *Foreign policy* 89 (1992): 3-20.

56. Jackson, Robert H., and Carl G. Rosberg. "Why Africa's weak states persist: The empirical and the juridical in statehood." *World politics* 35.1 (1982): 1-24.

57. Krasner, Stephen D. "Sharing sovereignty: New institutions for collapsed and failing states." *International Security* 29.2 (2004): 85-120.

58. Mansfield, Edward D., and Jack Snyder. "Democratization and War." *Foreign Affairs*. 74 (1995): 79.

59. Rubin, Barnett R. "Crafting a constitution for Afghanistan." *Journal of Democracy* 15.3 (2004): 5-19.

60. Siddique, Abubakar. "Afghanistan's ethnic divides", Barcelona Centre for International Affairs, January 2012.

61. Smith, Scott. "The Future of Afghan Democracy." *Stability: International Journal of Security and Development* 3.1: 12 (2014) pp. 1-9.

V. Scholarly Articles in Russian:

62. Афганистан. Население. Большая советская энциклопедия. 3-е изд. М.: «Большая советская энциклопедия». – 1970. – Т. 2. – с. 472.

63. Брагин А., Максимов И. «К вопросу о сущности понятия «Этнический конфликт» в условиях этнотрансформационных процессов». *Среднерусский вестник общественных наук* 2 (2009). стр. 53-62.

64. Лалетин Ю. П. Межэтническое взаимодействие в Афганистане //Конфликты на Востоке: этнические и конфессиональные/Под ред. АД Воскресенского.–М.: Аспект Пресс. – 2008. – с. 289-314.

65. Логинов А. В. Национальный вопрос в Афганистане // Расы и народы. М., 1990. с. 174.

66. Нессар О. «Боннская модель» и политический процесс в Афганистане в 2001–2004 гг. //Вестник Калмыцкого института гуманитарных исследований Российской академии наук. – 2016. – №. 1.

VI. International Reports:

67. Fragile States Index Annual Report 2019. The Fund for Peace (FFP). Available at: https://fragilestatesindex.org/wp-content/uploads/2019/03/9511904-fragilestatesindex.pdf

68. Institute for Economics & Peace. Global Peace Index 2018: Measuring Peace in a Complex World, Sydney, June 2018. Available at: http://visionofhumanity.org/reports

69. Institute for Economics & Peace. Global Terrorism Index 2018: Measuring the impact of terrorism, Sydney, November 2018. Available from: http://visionofhumanity.org/reports

70. Quarterly Report to the United States Congress // Special Inspector General for Afghanistan Reconstruction (SIGAR). January 30, 2017. p. 89. Available at:

https://www.sigar.mil/pdf/quarterlyreports/2017-01-30qr.pdf

71. Weinbaum, Marvin G. "Afghanistan, and its Neighbors, An Ever Dangerous Neighborhood" *Special Report* 162 (2006): 12. Available at: https://www.usip.org/sites/default/files/sr162.pdf

VII. Internet Sources:

72. Address by the President of the Republic of Uzbekistan Shavkat Mirziyoyev at the international conference on Afghanistan "Peace process, security cooperation and regional connectivity" March 27, 2018. Availableat: https://president.uz/en/lists/view/1601

73. "Afghanistan". Encyclopedia Britannica. Retrieved April 5, 2019. Availableat: https://www.britannica.com/place/Afghanistan

74. Constable P. Return of warlord Hekmatyar adds to Afghan political tensions // *The Washington Post*. May 21, 2017. Available at: https://www.washingtonpost.com/world/asia_pacific/return-of-warlord-hekmatyar-adds-to-afghan-political-

tensions/2017/05/18/1fa9fb20-398a-11e7-a59b-26e0451a96fd_story.html?utm_term=.22092001ffcf

75. Craig, Tim (21 September 2014). "Ghani named winner of Afghan election, will share power with rival in new government". *Washington Post*. Retrieved April 15, 2019. Available at: https://www.washingtonpost.com/world/ghani-abdullah-agree-to-share-power-in-afghanistan-as-election-stalemate-ends/2014/09/21/df58749a-416e-11e4-9a15-137aa0153527_story.html?noredirect=on&utm_term=.3fb6b1a935c6

76. Dearing M. Capture the Flag in Afghanistan // *Foreign Policy*. January 22, 2015. Available at: https://foreignpolicy.com/2015/01/22/capture-the-flag-in-afghanistan/

77. Gen. Dostum to probably return home, says Ghani. // *Pajhwok Afghan News*. July 15, 2018. URL: https://www.pajhwok.com/en/2018/07/15/gen-dostum-probably-return-home-says-ghani

78. Interviews - Dr. Abdullah Campaign Against Terror. Available at:

http://www.pbs.org/wgbh/pages/frontline/shows/campaign/interviews/abdullah.html

79. Karim Amini. New alliance lists demands; calls for systematic reforms// The Washington Post. May 21, 2017. URL: http://www.tolonews.com/afghanistan/new-alliance-lists-demands-calls-systematic-reforms

80. Mujib Mashal. 2 Weeks of U.S.-Taliban Talks End with "Progress" but No Breakthrough. *The New York Times*. March 12, 2019. Available at: https://www.nytimes.com/2019/03/12/world/asia/afghanistan-us-taliban-talks.html

81. President Shavkat Mirziyoyev addressed the 72nd Session of the United Nations General Assembly. September 20, 2017. Availableat: https://president.uz/en/lists/view/1063

82. Абдул Рашид Дустум провел переговоры с президентом Турции. 18 ноября 2017 г. [Электронный ресурс] // «Афганистан.Ру» – Информационный портал. Режим доступа: http://afghanistan.ru/doc/116561.html

83. Афганистан. Большая российская энциклопедия – [Электронная версия] / Режим обращения: http://bigenc.ru/geography/text/4053221

84. В Афганистане пытаются создать «Северный альянс 2.0». 12 июля 2017 г. [Электронный ресурс] // «PolitRUS» – Экспертно-аналитическая сеть. Режим доступа: http://www.politrus.com/2017/07/12/nord-alliance/

85. Выступление Президента Республики Узбекистан Шавката Мирзиёева на международной конференции «Центральная Азия: одно прошлое и общее будущее, сотрудничество ради устойчивого развития и взаимного процветания» в Самарканде. 10.11.2017 г. URL: https://president.uz/ru/lists/view/1227

86. Коргун В.Г. Состав афганского парламента. Институт Ближнего Востока. Режим обращения: https://www.iran.ru/news/analytics/36479/Sostav_afganskogo_parlamenta

87. Лидер ИПА Гульбеддин Хекматъяр подписал мирный договор с правительством. 29 сентября 2016 г. [Электронный ресурс] // «Афганистан сегодня» – Информационное

агентство. Режим доступа: http://www.afghanistantoday.ru/hovosti/lider-ipa-gulbeddin-hekmatyar.

88. Мохаммад Мохакик и Атта Мохаммад Нур обвинили президента в превышении полномочий. 9 июля 2018г. [Электронный ресурс] // «Афганистан.Ру» – Информационный портал. Режим доступа: http://afghanistan.ru/doc/116561.html .

89. НАТО начинает в Афганистане небоевую миссию "Решительная поддержка". 1 января 2015 г. [Электронный ресурс] // ТАСС – Информационное агентство России. Режим доступа: http://tass.ru/mezhdunarodnaya-panorama/1682351.

90. Срочно источник: Абдуррашид Дустум покинул Афганистан. 20 мая 2017 г. [Электронный ресурс] // «Афганистан сегодня» – Информационное агентство. Режим доступа: http://www.afghanistantoday.ru/hovosti/lider-ipa-gulbeddin-hekmatyar

APPENDICES

Table-1. The Share of Ethnic Groups in the Population of Afghanistan According to Data from Various Sources.

	Encyclopedia Britannica [124]	Afghanistan in 2012: A Survey of the Afghan People [125]	Great Russian Encyclopedia [126]	Great Soviet Encyclopedia (1970) [127]
Pashtuns	42 %	40 %	38-50 %	50 %
Tajiks	27 %	33 %	18-27 %	20 %
Hazaras	9 %	11 %	8-9 %	9 %
Uzbeks	9 %	9 %	6-9 %	9,5 %
Aimaq people	4 %	1 %	6 %	2,8 %
Turkmens	3 %	2 %	2,5 %	2 %
Others	6 %	4 %	-	6 %

---

[124] "Afghanistan". Encyclopedia Britannica. Retrieved June 5, 2017. URL: https://www.britannica.com /place/Afghanistan

[125] Hopkins, Nancy, ed. Afghanistan in 2012: A Survey of the Afghan People. AsiaFoundation, 2012.p. 182

[126] Афганистан. Большая российская энциклопедия – [Электронная версия] / Режим обращения: http://bigenc.ru/geography/text/4053221

[127] Афганистан. Население. Большая советская энциклопедия. 3-е изд. М.: «Большая советская энциклопедия». – 1970. – Т. 2. – с. 472.

Table-2. The Rank of Afghanistan in the International Indexes that Determines the Security of the Country and the Stability of Statehood Institutions.

No.	Index name	Rank of Afghanistan	Total number of countries, listed in the index
1.	Fragile States Index 2019[128]	9 (105.0 score)	178
2.	Global Peace Index 2018[129]	162 (3.585 scores)	163
3.	Global Terrorism Index 2018[130]	2 (9.391 score)	163

---

[128] Fragile States Index Annual Report 2019. The Fund for Peace (FFP). Available at: https://fragilestatesindex.org/wp-content/uploads/2019/03/9511904-fragilestatesindex.pdf

[129] Institute for Economics & Peace. Global Peace Index 2018: Measuring Peace in a Complex World, Sydney, June 2018. Available at: http://visionofhumanity.org/reports

[130] Institute for Economics & Peace. Global Terrorism Index 2018: Measuring the impact of terrorism, Sydney, November 2018. Availablefrom: http://visionofhumanity.org/reports

Table-3. Ethnic (Tribal) Affiliation of the Leaders of Afghanistan from 1747 to the Present Day.

Name	Title (status)	Reign (presidency)	Ethnicity	Tribal confederacy	Tribe
Durrani Empire (1747–1823)					
Ahmad Shah Durrani	Emir	1747-1772	Pashtun	Durrani (Abdali)	Popalzai (from the clan Sadozai)
Timur Shah Durrani		1772-1793			
Zaman Shah Durrani		1793-1801			
Mahmud Shah Durrani		1801-1803			
Shuja Shah Durrani		1803-1809			
Mahmud Shah Durrani		1809-1818			
Ali Shah Durrani		1818-1819			
Ayub Shah Durrani		1819-1823			
Emirate of Afghanistan (1823–1926)					
Dost Mohammad Khan	Emir	1823-1839	Pashtun	Durrani (Abdali)	Barakzai
Shuja Shah Durrani		1839-1842			Popalzai (from the clan Sadozai)
Akbar Khan		1842-1845			Barakzai

Name	Title	Reign	Ethnicity	Tribe	Clan
Dost Mohammad Khan		1845-1863			
Sher Ali Khan		1863-1865			
Mohammad Afzal Khan		1865-1867			
Mohammad Azam Khan		1867-1868			
Sher Ali Khan		1868-1879			
Ayub Khan		1879-1880			
Abdur Rahman Khan		1880-1901			
Habibullah Khan		1901-1919			
Amanullah Khan		1919-1926			
Kingdom of Afghanistan (1926–1973)					
Amanullah Khan	King	1926-1929	Pashtun	Durrani (Abdali)	Barakzai
Habibullah Kalakani	Emir (Usurper)	1929 (January - October)	Tajik		
Mohammed Nadir Shah	King	1929-1933	Pashtun	Durrani (Abdali)	Barakzai
Mohammed Zahir		1933-1973			

132

Shah					
Republic of Afghanistan (1973—1978)					
Mohammed Daoud Khan	President	1973-1978	Pashtun	Durrani (Abdali)	Barakzai
Democratic Republic of Afghanistan (1978—1987)					
Nur Muhammad Taraki	General Secretary of the CC of the PDPA; Chairman of the Revolutionary Council	1978-1979	Pashtun	Ghilji	Tarak (from the branch Buran)
Hafizullah Amin		1979 (September-December)	Pashtun	Ghilji	Kharoti
Babrak Karmal		1979-1986			Belonged to the tribe by mother
Republic of Afghanistan (1987-1992)					
Mohammad Najibullah	President	1987-1992	Pashtun	Ghilji	Sulaimankhel (from the clan Ahmadzai)
Islamic State of Afghanistan (1992-2001)					
Sibghatullah Mojaddedi	President	1992 (April-June)	Pashtun		
Burhanuddin Rabbani		1992-2001	Tajik		
Islamic Emirate of Afghanistan (1996-2001)					
Mohammed Omar	Amir al-Mu'minin	1996-2001	Pashtun	Ghilji	Hotak
Islamic Republic of Afghanistan (2001-present)					

133

Hamid Karzai	Chairman of the Interim Administration; Chairman of a transitional administration; President	2001-2002	Pashtun	Durrani (Abdali)	Popalzai (from the clan Karzai)[131]
		2002-2004			
		2004-2014			
Ashraf Ghani	President	2014-presently	Pashtun	Ghilji	Sulaimankhel (from the clan Ahmadzai)[132]

---

[131] Туляганова Н.У. Афганский фактор в современных международных отношениях в Центральной Азии. Ташкент: Фан, 2004, 211 с.

[132] See: Lee, Jonathan L. *Afghanistan: A History from 1260 to the Present.* Reaktion Books, 2018.

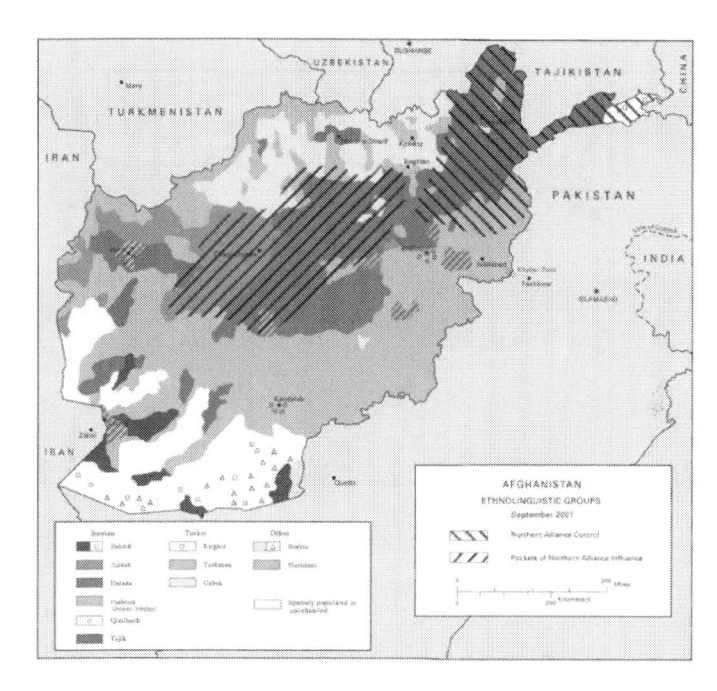

Map 1. Ethno-linguistic groups in Afghanistan (September 2001)

Source: US Army ethnolinguistic map of Afghanistan - circa 2001-09. United States Army Center of Military History. Available at: https://history.army.mil/brochures/Afghanistan/Operation%20Enduring%20Freedom.htm

Map 2. Afghanistan Tribes. Pashtun Tribal Confederacies in Afghanistan and Pakistan

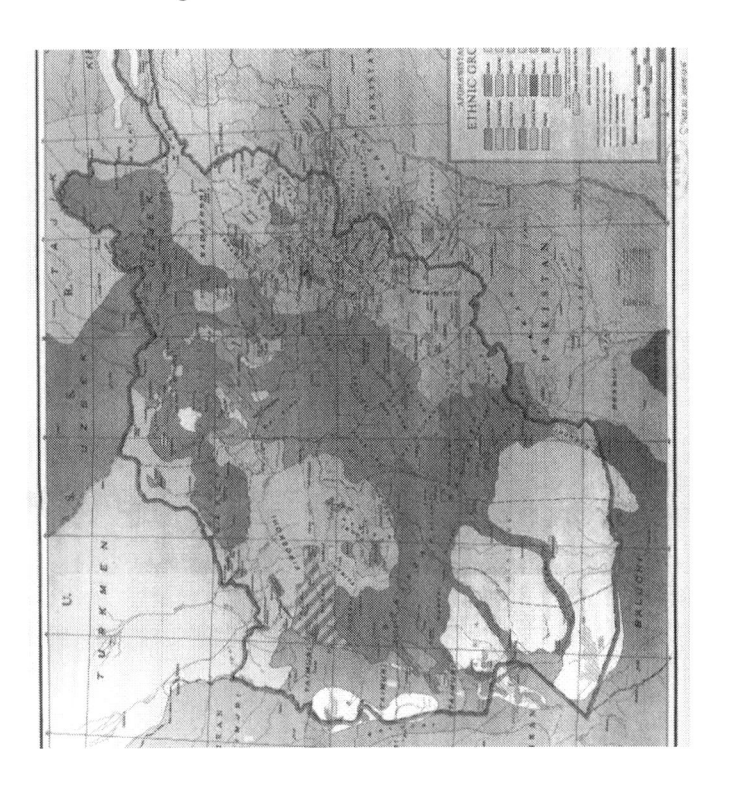

Source: CIA map showing the territory of the settlement of ethnic groups and subgroups in Afghanistan. Scale ca. 1:22,000 (E 600--E 740/N 380--N 300). United States Library of Congress's Geography and Map Division. Available at: http://hdl.loc.gov/loc.gmd/g7631e.ct002134

Map 3. Provinces of Afghanistan in 1929

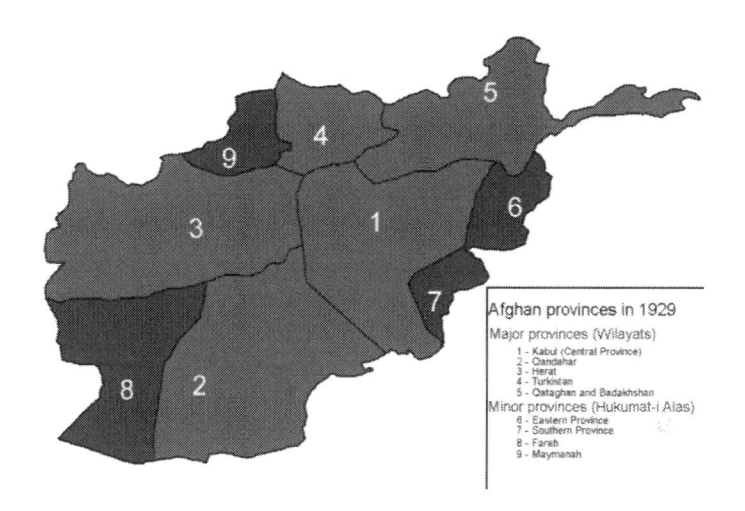

Source: Provinces of Afghanistan in 1929. Adapted from Page XII of "Kabul Under Siege: Fayz Muhammad's Account of the 1929 Uprising". Available at: https://upload.wikimedia.org/wikipedia/commons/6/63/Provinces_of_Afghanistan_in_1929.png

Map 4. Provinces of Afghanistan, 1964

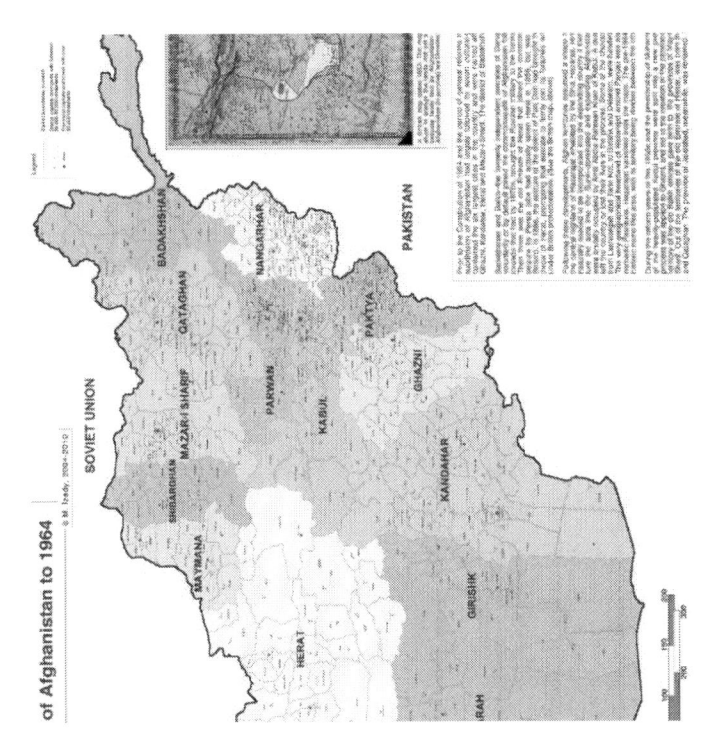

Source: Dr. Michael Izady. Atlas of the Islamic World and Vicinity. The Gulf/2000 Project – SIPA – Columbia University. Available at: http://gulf2000.columbia.edu/images/maps/AfghanistanProvincial_1964_lg.jpg

This page is intentionally left blank.

NOTES:

Printed in Great Britain
by Amazon